Financial Services Act Companies Act 2010

Text and Guidelines

ISBN/EAN: 9783867413725

© Europaeischer Hochschulverlag GmbH & Co KG,

Fahrenheitstr. 1, D-28359 Bremen (www.ehv-online.com).

Financial Services Act 2010

CHAPTER 28

CONTENTS

Objectives of FSA etc

1 Financial stability objective
2 Enhancing public understanding of financial matters etc
3 Meeting FSA's regulatory objectives

Remuneration of executives of authorised persons

4 Executives' remuneration reports
5 Executives' remuneration reports: supplementary
6 Rules made by FSA about remuneration

Recovery and resolution plans

7 Rules made by FSA about recovery and resolution plans

Short selling

8 Power of FSA to prohibit, or require disclosure of, short selling

FSA's disciplinary powers

9 Suspending permission to carry on regulated activities etc
10 Removal of restriction on imposing a penalty and cancelling authorisation
11 Performance of controlled function without approval
12 Approved persons guilty of misconduct
13 Publication of decision notices

Measures to protect consumers

14 Consumer redress schemes
15 Restrictions on provision of credit card cheques

Financial Services Compensation Scheme

16 Contribution to costs of special resolution regime
17 Power to require FSCS manager to act in relation to other schemes

Powers to require information

18 Information relating to financial stability
19 Asset protection scheme etc

Banking Act 2009

20 Services forming part of recognised inter-bank payment systems
21 Minor amendments of provision made by Banking Act 2009

Director of Savings

22 Administration of court funds by Director of Savings

General

23 Orders or regulations
24 Minor and consequential amendments
25 Extent
26 Commencement
27 Short title

Schedule 1 — Further provision about the consumer financial education body
Schedule 2 — Minor and consequential amendments
    Part 1 — Amendments of Financial Services and Markets Act 2000
    Part 2 — Amendments of other legislation

Financial Services Act 2010

2010 CHAPTER 28

An Act to make provision amending the Financial Services and Markets Act 2000, including provision about financial education, and other provision about financial services and markets; and to make provision for the administration of court funds by the Director of Savings.   [8th April 2010]

B E IT ENACTED by the Queen's most Excellent Majesty, by and with the advice and consent of the Lords Spiritual and Temporal, and Commons, in this present Parliament assembled, and by the authority of the same, as follows:—

Objectives of FSA etc

1 Financial stability objective

(1) The Financial Services and Markets Act 2000 is amended as follows.

(2) In section 2(2) (the FSA's regulatory objectives), after paragraph (a) insert—
"(ab) financial stability;".

(3) After section 3 insert—

"**3A Financial stability**

(1) The financial stability objective is: contributing to the protection and enhancement of the stability of the UK financial system.

(2) In considering that objective the Authority must have regard to—
   (a) the economic and fiscal consequences for the United Kingdom of instability of the UK financial system;
   (b) the effects (if any) on the growth of the economy of the United Kingdom of anything done for the purpose of meeting that objective; and
   (c) the impact (if any) on the stability of the UK financial system of events or circumstances outside the United Kingdom (as well as in the United Kingdom).

(3) The Authority must, consulting the Treasury, determine and review its strategy in relation to the financial stability objective."

2 Enhancing public understanding of financial matters etc

(1) The Financial Services and Markets Act 2000 is amended as follows.

(2) In section 2 (the FSA's general duties) —
   (a) in subsection (2) (the FSA's regulatory objectives), omit paragraph (b) (which provides that public awareness is one of those objectives), and
   (b) in subsection (3) (matters to which FSA must have regard in discharging its general functions), after paragraph (g) insert —
      "(h) the desirability of enhancing the understanding and knowledge of members of the public of financial matters (including the UK financial system)."

(3) Omit section 4 (public awareness).

(4) In section 5(2) (the protection of consumers), after paragraph (b) insert —
      "(ba) any information which the consumer financial education body has provided to the Authority in the exercise of the consumer financial education function;".

(5) After section 6 insert —

"Enhancing public understanding of financial matters etc

6A Enhancing public understanding of financial matters etc

(1) The Authority must establish a body corporate ("the consumer financial education body") whose function ("the consumer financial education function") is to enhance —
   (a) the understanding and knowledge of members of the public of financial matters (including the UK financial system); and
   (b) the ability of members of the public to manage their own financial affairs.

(2) The consumer financial education function includes, in particular —
   (a) promoting awareness of the benefits of financial planning;
   (b) promoting awareness of the financial advantages and disadvantages in relation to the supply of particular kinds of goods or services;
   (c) promoting awareness of the benefits and risks associated with different kinds of financial dealing (which includes informing the Authority and other bodies of those benefits and risks);
   (d) the publication of educational materials or the carrying out of other educational activities; and
   (e) the provision of information and advice to members of the public.

(3) Schedule 1A makes further provision about the consumer financial education body."

(6) After Schedule 1 insert the Schedule 1A set out in Schedule 1 to this Act.

(7) If members of staff of the FSA are transferred to the consumer financial education body, the transfer is to be regarded for the purposes of TUPE as a relevant transfer, whether or not it would otherwise be so regarded.

(8) In subsection (7)—
"the consumer financial education body" has the same meaning as in section 6A of the Financial Services and Markets Act 2000,
"the FSA" means the Financial Services Authority, and
"TUPE" means the Transfer of Undertakings (Protection of Employment) Regulations 2006.

3 Meeting FSA's regulatory objectives

(1) The Financial Services and Markets Act 2000 is amended as follows.

(2) In section 44(3) (refusal of application by authorised person to vary or cancel its Part IV permission), for the words from "to it—" to the end substitute "to it that it is desirable to refuse the application in order to meet any of its regulatory objectives."

(3) In section 45 (variation or cancellation of Part IV permissions: FSA's own-initiative power)—
　　(a) in subsection (1), for paragraph (c) substitute—
　　　　"(c) it is desirable to exercise the power in order to meet any of its regulatory objectives.", and
　　(b) after that subsection insert—
　　　　"(1A) For the purposes of subsection (1)(c) it does not matter whether there is a relationship between the authorised person and the persons whose interests will be protected by the exercise of the power under this section."

(4) In section 138(1) and (1A) (general rule-making power), for "protecting the interests of consumers" substitute "meeting any of its regulatory objectives".

(5) In section 194 (general grounds on which power of intervention is exercisable)—
　　(a) in subsection (1), for paragraph (c) substitute—
　　　　"(c) it is desirable to exercise the power in order to meet any of its regulatory objectives.", and
　　(b) after that subsection insert—
　　　　"(1A) For the purposes of subsection (1)(c) it does not matter whether there is a relationship between the incoming firm and the persons whose interests will be protected by the exercise of the power of intervention."

Remuneration of executives of authorised persons

4 Executives' remuneration reports

(1) The Treasury may make provision by regulations about the preparation, approval and disclosure of executives' remuneration reports.

(2) An executives' remuneration report is a report containing information about—

(a) the remuneration of relevant executives of an authorised person, or
(b) anything connected with the remuneration of relevant executives of an authorised person.

(3) The following are relevant executives of an authorised person—
   (a) officers of the authorised person,
   (b) employees of the authorised person who fall within a prescribed description, and
   (c) other individuals who have a prescribed connection with the authorised person.

(4) The individuals who may fall within subsection (3)(c) include any description of—
   (a) individuals who provide services, or whose services are provided (directly or indirectly), to the authorised person, or
   (b) individuals who are officers or employees of a member of the same group as the authorised person.

(5) Regulations under this section may apply in relation to a prescribed description of authorised person.

(6) Regulations under this section are subject to affirmative resolution procedure.

5 Executives' remuneration reports: supplementary

(1) Regulations under section 4 may, in particular, make provision as to—
   (a) the information that must be contained in an executives' remuneration report,
   (b) how information is to be set out in the report, and
   (c) what is to be the auditable part of the report.

(2) The information that may be required to be contained in an executives' remuneration report includes—
   (a) information corresponding to information that could be required by regulations under section 421 of the Companies Act 2006 to be contained in a directors' remuneration report, and
   (b) information comparing the remuneration of relevant executives of an authorised person with the remuneration of employees of the authorised person who fall within a prescribed description.

(3) Regulations under section 4 may, in particular, make provision —
   (a) for the filing of executives' remuneration reports with the registrar of companies for any part of the United Kingdom or with the FSA, and
   (b) for the publication by the FSA of reports filed with it.

(4) Regulations under section 4 may apply any provision made by or under the Companies Act 2006 relating to directors' remuneration reports, subject to such exceptions, adaptations and modifications as the Treasury consider appropriate.

(5) The provisions that may be applied include provisions creating offences; but the regulations may not impose a liability for an offence which is more onerous than the liability for the offence under the applied provision.

(6) Regulations under section 4 may provide that any requirement imposed on an authorised person by the regulations is to be treated for the purposes of

prescribed provisions of the Financial Services and Markets Act 2000 as if it had been imposed on the person by a provision of that Act.

(7) For the purposes of section 4 and this section —

"authorised person" has the same meaning as in the Financial Services and Markets Act 2000 (see section 31),

"the FSA" means the Financial Services Authority,

"group" has the same meaning as in the Financial Services and Markets Act 2000 (see section 421),

"officer" —
- (a) in relation to a partnership, means a partner, and
- (b) in relation to a body corporate whose affairs are managed by its members, means a member, and

"prescribed" means specified in, or determined in accordance with, regulations under section 4.

6 Rules made by FSA about remuneration

In the Financial Services and Markets Act 2000, after section 139 insert —

"139A General rules about remuneration

(1) The Authority must exercise its power to make general rules so as to make rules requiring each authorised person (or each authorised person of a specified description) to have, and act in accordance with, a remuneration policy.

(2) A "remuneration policy" is a policy about the remuneration by the authorised person of —
- (a) officers,
- (b) employees, and
- (c) other persons,

of a specified description.

(3) The rules must secure that any remuneration policy that an authorised person is required by the rules to have is consistent with —
- (a) the effective management of risks; and
- (b) the Implementation Standards.

(4) When making rules about remuneration policies, the Authority must have regard to any other international standards about the remuneration of individuals working in the financial sector (or certain such individuals).

(5) The Treasury may direct the Authority to consider whether the remuneration policies of authorised persons specified in the direction (or of authorised persons of a description so specified) comply with requirements imposed by the rules as to the contents of the policies.

(6) Before giving a direction under subsection (5), the Treasury must consult the Authority.

(7) If the Authority considers that a remuneration policy fails to make provision which complies with the requirements mentioned in subsection (5), the Authority must take such steps as it considers appropriate to deal with the failure.

(8) The steps that the Authority may take include requiring the remuneration policy to be revised.

(9) General rules may—
   (a) prohibit persons (or persons of a specified description) from being remunerated in a specified way;
   (b) provide that any provision of an agreement that contravenes such a prohibition is void; and
   (c) provide for the recovery of any payment made, or other property transferred, in pursuance of a provision that is void by virtue of paragraph (b).

(10) A prohibition may be imposed under subsection (9)(a) only for the purpose of ensuring that the provision of remuneration is consistent with—
   (a) the effective management of risks; or
   (b) the Implementation Standards.

(11) A provision that, at the time the rules are made, is contained in an agreement made before that time may not be rendered void under subsection (9)(b) unless it is subsequently amended so as to contravene a prohibition under subsection (9)(a).

(12) In this section—
   "the Implementation Standards" means the Implementation Standards for Principles for Sound Compensation Practices, issued by the Financial Stability Board on 25 September 2009; and
   "specified" (except in subsection (5)) means specified by the rules.

(13) References to the Implementation Standards or to international standards of a kind mentioned in subsection (4) are to standards that are for the time being in force."

Recovery and resolution plans

7 **Rules made by FSA about recovery and resolution plans**

(1) In the Financial Services and Markets Act 2000, after section 139A (which is inserted by section 6 above) insert—

"**139B Rules about recovery plans**

(1) The Authority must exercise its power to make general rules so as to make rules requiring each authorised person (or each authorised person of a specified description) to prepare, and keep up-to-date, a recovery plan.

(2) A "recovery plan" is a document containing information within subsection (3) or (4) of a specified description.

(3) Information is within this subsection if it relates to action to be taken to secure that, in the event of specified circumstances affecting the carrying on of the business (or any part of the business) of the authorised person—
   (a) the business of the authorised person, or

(b) a specified part of the business of the authorised person,

is capable of being carried on (whether or not by the authorised person and whether or not in the same way as previously).

(4) Information is within this subsection if it would facilitate the carrying on of the business (or any part of the business) of the authorised person by any other person.

(5) The Authority must consider whether each recovery plan makes satisfactory provision in relation to the matters required by the rules to be covered by the plan.

(6) If the Authority considers that a recovery plan fails to make satisfactory provision in relation to any such matter, the Authority must take such steps as it considers appropriate to deal with the failure.

(7) The steps that the Authority may take include requiring the recovery plan to be revised.

(8) The authorised persons subject to general rules about recovery plans must include authorised persons in relation to whom any power under Part 1 of the Banking Act 2009 (special resolution regime) is exercisable.

(9) Before preparing a draft of general rules about recovery plans having effect in relation to those persons, the Authority must consult —
   (a) the Treasury; and
   (b) the Bank of England.

139C Rules about resolution plans

(1) The Authority must exercise its power to make general rules so as to make rules requiring each authorised person (or each authorised person of a specified description) to prepare, and keep up-to-date, a resolution plan.

(2) A "resolution plan" is a document containing information within subsection (3) or (4) of a specified description.

(3) Information is within this subsection if it relates to action to be taken in the event of —
   (a) circumstances arising in which it is likely that the business (or any part of the business) of the authorised person will fail; or
   (b) the failure of the business (or any part of the business) of the authorised person.

(4) Information is within this subsection if it would facilitate anything falling to be done by any person in consequence of that failure.

(5) An example of information within subsection (4) is information that, in the event of that failure, would facilitate —
   (a) planning by the Treasury in relation to the possible exercise of any of their powers under Part 1 of the Banking Act 2009; or
   (b) planning by the Bank of England in relation to the possible exercise of any of its powers under Part 1, 2 or 3 of that Act.

(6) The Authority must consider whether each resolution plan makes satisfactory provision in relation to the matters required by the rules to be covered by the plan.

(7) If the Authority considers that a resolution plan fails to make satisfactory provision in relation to any such matter, the Authority must take such steps as it considers appropriate to deal with the failure.

(8) The steps that the Authority may take include requiring the resolution plan to be revised.

(9) The authorised persons subject to general rules about resolution plans must include authorised persons in relation to whom any power under Part 1 of the Banking Act 2009 is exercisable.

(10) Before preparing a draft of general rules about resolution plans having effect in relation to those persons, the Authority must consult—
  (a) the Treasury; and
  (b) the Bank of England.

139D Sections 139B and 139C: interpretation

(1) In sections 139B and 139C any reference to the taking of action includes the taking of action by—
  (a) the authorised person;
  (b) any other person in the same group as the authorised person; or
  (c) a partnership of which the authorised person is a member.

(2) In subsection (1)(b) the definition of "group" in section 421 applies with the omission of subsection (1)(e) and (f) of that section.

(3) For the purposes of section 139C the cases in which the business (or any part of the business) of the authorised person is to be regarded as having failed include—
  (a) the insolvency or bankruptcy of the authorised person;
  (b) the authorised person entering into administration; and
  (c) a power under Part 1 of the Banking Act 2009 being exercised in relation to the authorised person.

(4) In sections 139B and 139C references to the business of an authorised person include the business of—
  (a) any person in the same group as the authorised person; and
  (b) a partnership of which the authorised person is a member;
and, accordingly, references in subsection (3)(a) to (c) of this section to the authorised person include any person within paragraph (a) or (b).

(5) In sections 139B and 139C "specified" means specified in general rules.

(6) In this section—
  "administration" includes administration under Part 3 of the Banking Act 2009;
  "insolvency" includes insolvency under Part 2 of that Act.

139E Rules about recovery and resolution plans: supplementary provision

(1) General rules about recovery or resolution plans may, in particular—
  (a) impose a requirement on authorised persons to collect, and keep up-to-date, information of a description specified in the rules; and

(b) make provision as to the inclusion in the plans of information in respect of the steps to be taken to ensure compliance with that requirement.

(2) If the Authority considers that an authorised person has contravened that requirement, the Authority may require the authorised person to appoint a skilled person to collect or update the information in question.

(3) References in this section to a skilled person are to a person —
   (a) nominated or approved by the Authority; and
   (b) appearing to the Authority to have the skills necessary to collect or update the information in question.

(4) The skilled person may require any person to provide all such assistance as the skilled person may reasonably require to collect or update the information in question.

(5) A requirement imposed by subsection (4) is enforceable, on the application of the Authority, by an injunction or, in Scotland, by an order for specific performance under section 45 of the Court of Session Act 1988.

(6) A contractual or other requirement imposed on a person ("P") to keep any information in confidence does not apply if —
   (a) the information is or may be relevant to anything required to be done as a result of section 139B or 139C or this section;
   (b) an authorised person or a skilled person requests or requires P to provide the information for the purpose of securing that those things are done; and
   (c) the Authority has approved the making of the request or the imposition of the requirement before it is made or imposed.

(7) An authorised person may provide information (whether received under subsection (6) or otherwise) that would otherwise be subject to a contractual or other requirement to keep in confidence if it is provided for the purposes of anything required to be done as a result of section 139B or 139C or this section.

(8) General rules about recovery or resolution plans may, in particular, make provision about the form of the plans.

(9) When making general rules about recovery or resolution plans, the Authority must have regard to any international standards about documents whose purpose corresponds to the purpose of recovery or resolution plans.

139F Special provision in relation to resolution plans

(1) In the case of resolution plans required to be prepared by general rules, the Authority must consult —
   (a) the Treasury, and
   (b) the Bank of England ("the Bank"),
about the adequacy of the plans so far as relating to any matter which may be relevant to the exercise by the Treasury or the Bank of any power under Part 1, 2 or 3 of the Banking Act 2009.

(2) After being consulted under subsection (1) —
   (a) the Treasury or the Bank may notify the Authority that, in the opinion of the Treasury or the Bank, a resolution plan fails to make satisfactory provision in relation to any such matter; and
   (b) if the Treasury or the Bank give a notification under paragraph (a), the Treasury or the Bank must give reasons for being of that opinion to the Authority.

(3) The Authority must have regard to any notification given under paragraph (a) of subsection (2) before considering whether any resolution plan makes satisfactory provision in relation to any such matter.

(4) If —
   (a) a notification is given under that paragraph, but
   (b) the Authority is nonetheless of the opinion that the resolution plan makes satisfactory provision in relation to any such matter,
   the Authority must give reasons for being of that opinion to the person who gave the notification."

(2) The Treasury may by order require the FSA to make, by a date specified in the order, recovery plan rules, or resolution plan rules, which impose requirements on authorised persons who are of a description specified in the order.

(3) Before making an order under subsection (2), the Treasury must consult the FSA.

(4) An order under subsection (2) is subject to negative resolution procedure.

(5) In this section —
   "the FSA" means the Financial Services Authority,
   "recovery plan rules" means general rules imposing requirements of a kind mentioned in section 139B(1) of the Financial Services and Markets Act 2000, and
   "resolution plan rules" means general rules imposing requirements of a kind mentioned in section 139C(1) of that Act.

Short selling

8 Power of FSA to prohibit, or require disclosure of, short selling

In the Financial Services and Markets Act 2000, after Part 8 insert —

"PART 8A

SHORT SELLING

Short selling rules

131B Short selling rules

(1) The Authority may make rules prohibiting in specified cases persons from engaging in short selling in relation to relevant financial

instruments (or relevant financial instruments of a specified description).

(2) The Authority may make rules requiring—
  (a) a person who has engaged in short selling in relation to relevant financial instruments (or relevant financial instruments of a specified description), or
  (b) an authorised person of a specified description who has acted on behalf of such a person,
  to disclose in specified cases specified information, or information of a specified description, about the short selling.

(3) Rules under subsection (2) may specify the time by which, and the way in which, the disclosure must be made (and may in particular provide for the information to be disclosed to the Authority or published in a specified way).

(4) Rules under subsection (2) may apply in relation to short selling engaged in before the rules are made where the resulting short position is still open when the rules are made.

(5) The reference to a short position being open is to be read in accordance with provision made by the rules.

(6) Rules under this section may apply to short selling wholly outside the United Kingdom by persons outside the United Kingdom, but only in so far as the rules relate to UK financial instruments.

(7) The description of relevant financial instruments that may be specified by the rules includes relevant financial instruments issued by a specified person.

(8) Rules under this section are referred to in this Part as "short selling rules".

(9) The Authority must, when making short selling rules, have regard to any international agreement as to measures to be taken in respect of short selling.

131C Short selling rules: definitions etc

(1) This section supplements section 131B.

(2) The cases in which a person ("S") engages in short selling in relation to a financial instrument (a "shorted instrument") include any case where—
  (a) S enters into a transaction which creates, or relates to, another financial instrument; and
  (b) the effect (or one of the effects) of the transaction is to confer a financial advantage on S in the event of a decrease in the price or value of the shorted instrument.

(3) "Financial instrument" has the meaning given by Article 4.1(17) of the markets in financial instruments directive.

(4) "Relevant financial instrument" means a financial instrument that—
  (a) is admitted to trading on a regulated market or on any other prescribed market in an EEA State; or

(b) has such other connection with a market in an EEA State as may be specified.

(5) "Specified" means specified by short selling rules.

(6) "UK financial instrument" means a financial instrument that is admitted to trading on a market in the United Kingdom.

(7) In the case of a financial instrument that is admitted to trading on—
   (a) a market in the United Kingdom or another EEA State, and
   (b) one or more markets in a country or territory, or countries or territories, anywhere else in the world,
short selling rules may apply in relation to trading on both or all markets.

(8) In any case where—
   (a) a financial instrument ("instrument A") is admitted to trading on a market in the United Kingdom or another EEA State,
   (b) another financial instrument ("instrument B") is admitted to trading on one or more markets in a country or territory, or countries or territories, anywhere else in the world, and
   (c) the price or value of instrument A depends on the price or value of instrument B (or vice versa),
short selling rules may apply in relation to trading on both or all markets.

(9) In subsection (4)(a) "regulated market" has the meaning given by Article 4.1(14) of the markets in financial instruments directive.

(10) References in this section to a market in a country or territory are to a market situated or operating in the country or territory.

131D Short selling rules: procedure in urgent cases

(1) The Authority may make short selling rules (and may subsequently amend those rules) without complying with section 155 (consultation in relation to proposed rules) if it considers that it is necessary to do so, in order to—
   (a) maintain confidence in the UK financial system; or
   (b) protect the stability of the UK financial system.

(2) Any rules made by virtue of subsection (1) ("emergency rules") cease to have effect at the end of the period of three months beginning with the day on which the rules are made ("the relevant day"); but this is subject as follows.

(3) The Authority may direct that emergency rules are to cease to have effect at the end of a period (not exceeding six months beginning with the relevant day) specified in the direction.

(4) A direction under subsection (3) may be made only if, immediately before the end of the period mentioned in subsection (2), the Authority considers that it is necessary to do so, in order to—
   (a) maintain confidence in the UK financial system; or
   (b) protect the stability of the UK financial system.

(5) Such a direction must be published by the Authority in the way appearing to the Authority to be best calculated to bring it to the attention of the public.

(6) Nothing in subsection (2) or (3) prevents the Authority from revoking emergency rules before the end of the periods referred to there.

Power to require information

131E Power to require information

(1) The Authority may, by notice in writing, require a person ("P") —
   (a) to provide specified information or information of a specified description; or
   (b) to produce specified documents or documents of a specified description.

(2) This section applies only to information and documents that the Authority reasonably requires for the purpose of determining whether P, or a person connected with P, has contravened any provision of short selling rules.

(3) Information or documents required under this section must be provided or produced —
   (a) before the end of such reasonable period as may be specified; and
   (b) at such place as may be specified.

(4) The Authority may require any information provided under this section to be provided in such form as it may reasonably require.

(5) The Authority may require —
   (a) any information provided, whether in a document or otherwise, to be verified in such manner as it may reasonably require; or
   (b) any document produced to be authenticated in such manner as it may reasonably require.

(6) In this section "specified" means specified in the notice.

(7) For the purposes of this section a person is connected with another person ("P") if the person is or has at any relevant time been —
   (a) a member of P's group;
   (b) a controller of P;
   (c) any other member of a partnership of which P is a member; or
   (d) in relation to P, a person mentioned in Part 1 of Schedule 15 (reading references in that Part to the authorised person as references to P).

131F Power to require information: supplementary

(1) If the Authority has power under section 131E to require a person to produce a document but it appears that the document is in the possession of a third person, that power may be exercised in relation to the third person.

(2) If a document is produced in response to a requirement imposed under section 131E, the Authority may —

(a) take copies of or extracts from the document; or
(b) require the person producing the document, or any relevant person, to provide an explanation of the document.

(3) In subsection (2)(b) "relevant person", in relation to a person who is required to produce a document, means a person who —
   (a) has been or is or is proposed to be a director or controller of that person;
   (b) has been or is an auditor of that person;
   (c) has been or is an actuary, accountant or lawyer appointed or instructed by that person; or
   (d) has been or is an employee of that person.

(4) If a person who is required under section 131E to produce a document fails to do so, the Authority may require the person to state, to the best of the person's knowledge and belief, where the document is.

(5) A lawyer may be required under section 131E to provide the name and address of the lawyer's client.

(6) A person ("P") may not be required under section 131E to disclose information or produce a document in respect of which P owes an obligation of confidence by virtue of carrying on the business of banking unless —
   (a) P is the person under investigation or a member of that person's group;
   (b) the person to whom the obligation of confidence is owed is the person under investigation or a member of that person's group; or
   (c) the person to whom the obligation of confidence is owed consents to the disclosure or production.

(7) If a person claims a lien on a document, its production under section 131E does not affect the lien.

Breach of short selling rules etc

131G Power to impose penalty or issue censure

(1) This section applies if the Authority is satisfied that a person has contravened —
   (a) any provision of short selling rules; or
   (b) any requirement imposed on the person under section 131E or 131F.

(2) The Authority may impose a penalty of such amount as it considers appropriate on —
   (a) the person who contravened the provision or requirement; or
   (b) any person who was knowingly concerned in the contravention.

(3) It may, instead of imposing a penalty on a person, publish a statement censuring the person.

(4) The Authority may not take action against a person under this section after the end of the limitation period unless, before the end of that period, it has given a warning notice to the person under section 131H.

(5) "The limitation period" means the period of three years beginning with the first day on which the Authority knew of the contravention.

(6) For this purpose the Authority is to be treated as knowing of a contravention if it has information from which the contravention can reasonably be inferred.

131H Procedure and right to refer to Tribunal

(1) If the Authority proposes to take action against a person under section 131G, it must give the person a warning notice.

(2) A warning notice about a proposal to impose a penalty must state the amount of the penalty.

(3) A warning notice about a proposal to publish a statement must set out the terms of the statement.

(4) If the Authority decides to take action against a person under section 131G, it must give the person a decision notice.

(5) A decision notice about the imposition of a penalty must state the amount of the penalty.

(6) A decision notice about the publication of a statement must set out the terms of the statement.

(7) If the Authority decides to take action against a person under section 131G, the person may refer the matter to the Tribunal.

131I Duty on publication of statement

After a statement under section 131G(3) is published, the Authority must send a copy of the statement to —
   (a) the person in respect of whom it is made; and
   (b) any person to whom a copy of the decision notice was given under section 393(4).

131J Imposition of penalties under section 131G: statement of policy

(1) The Authority must prepare and issue a statement of its policy with respect to —
   (a) the imposition of penalties under section 131G; and
   (b) the amount of penalties under that section.

(2) The Authority's policy in determining what the amount of a penalty should be must include having regard to —
   (a) the seriousness of the contravention;
   (b) the extent to which the contravention was deliberate or reckless; and
   (c) whether the person on whom the penalty is to be imposed is an individual.

(3) The Authority may at any time alter or replace a statement issued under this section.

(4) If a statement issued under this section is altered or replaced, the Authority must issue the altered or replaced statement.

(5) The Authority must, without delay, give the Treasury a copy of any statement which it publishes under this section.

(6) A statement issued under this section must be published by the Authority in the way appearing to the Authority to be best calculated to bring it to the attention of the public.

(7) The Authority may charge a reasonable fee for providing a person with a copy of the statement.

(8) In exercising, or deciding whether to exercise, a power under section 131G in the case of any particular contravention, the Authority must have regard to any statement of policy published under this section and in force at a time when the contravention occurred.

131K Statement of policy: procedure

(1) Before issuing a statement under section 131J, the Authority must publish a draft of the proposed statement in the way appearing to the Authority to be best calculated to bring it to the attention of the public.

(2) The draft must be accompanied by notice that representations about the proposal may be made to the Authority within a specified time.

(3) Before issuing the proposed statement, the Authority must have regard to any representations made to it in accordance with subsection (2).

(4) If the Authority issues the proposed statement it must publish an account, in general terms, of —
   (a) the representations made to it in accordance with subsection (2); and
   (b) its response to them.

(5) If the statement differs from the draft published under subsection (1) in a way which is, in the opinion of the Authority, significant, the Authority must (in addition to complying with subsection (4)) publish details of the difference.

(6) The Authority may charge a reasonable fee for providing a person with a copy of a draft published under subsection (1).

(7) This section also applies to a proposal to alter or replace a statement."

FSA's disciplinary powers

9 **Suspending permission to carry on regulated activities etc**

In Part 14 of the Financial Services and Markets Act 2000 (disciplinary measures), after section 206 insert —

"206A Suspending permission to carry on regulated activities etc

(1) If the Authority considers that an authorised person has contravened a relevant requirement imposed on the person, it may —

(a) suspend, for such period as it considers appropriate, any permission which the person has to carry on a regulated activity; or

(b) impose, for such period as it considers appropriate, such limitations or other restrictions in relation to the carrying on of a regulated activity by the person as it considers appropriate.

(2) In subsection (1) —

"permission" means any permission that the authorised person has, whether given (or treated as given) by the Authority or conferred by any provision of this Act;

"relevant requirement" means a requirement imposed —
   (a) by or under this Act; or
   (b) by any directly applicable Community regulation made under the markets in financial instruments directive.

(3) The period for which a suspension or restriction is to have effect may not exceed 12 months.

(4) A suspension may relate only to the carrying on of an activity in specified circumstances.

(5) A restriction may, in particular, be imposed so as to require the person concerned to take, or refrain from taking, specified action.

(6) The Authority may —
   (a) withdraw a suspension or restriction; or
   (b) vary a suspension or restriction so as to reduce the period for which it has effect or otherwise to limit its effect.

(7) The power under this section may (but need not) be exercised so as to have effect in relation to all the regulated activities that the person concerned carries on.

(8) Any one or more of the powers under —
   (a) subsection (1)(a) and (b) of this section, and
   (b) sections 205 and 206,
may be exercised in relation to the same contravention."

10 Removal of restriction on imposing a penalty and cancelling authorisation

In section 206 of the Financial Services and Markets Act 2000 (financial penalties), omit subsection (2) (which prevents the FSA from imposing a penalty under that section as well as withdrawing a person's authorisation under section 33).

11 Performance of controlled function without approval

In the Financial Services and Markets Act 2000, after section 63 insert —

"*Performance of controlled functions without approval*

63A Power to impose penalties

(1) If the Authority is satisfied that —

(a) a person ("P") has at any time performed a controlled function without approval, and
(b) at that time P knew, or could reasonably be expected to have known, that P was performing a controlled function without approval,

it may impose a penalty on P of such amount as it considers appropriate.

(2) For the purposes of this section P performs a controlled function without approval at any time if at that time —
  (a) P performs a controlled function under an arrangement entered into by an authorised person ("A"), or by a contractor of A, in relation to the carrying on by A of a regulated activity; and
  (b) the performance by P of the function was not approved under section 59.

(3) The Authority may not impose a penalty under this section after the end of the limitation period unless, before the end of that period, it has given a warning notice to the person concerned under section 63B(1).

(4) "The limitation period" means the period of three years beginning with the first day on which the Authority knew that the person concerned had performed a controlled function without approval.

(5) For this purpose the Authority is to be treated as knowing that a person has performed a controlled function without approval if it has information from which that can reasonably be inferred.

(6) Any expression which is used both in this section and section 59 has the same meaning in this section as in that section.

63B Procedure and right to refer to Tribunal

(1) If the Authority proposes to impose a penalty on a person under section 63A, it must give the person a warning notice.

(2) A warning notice must state the amount of the penalty.

(3) If the Authority decides to impose a penalty on a person under section 63A, it must give the person a decision notice.

(4) A decision notice must state the amount of the penalty.

(5) If the Authority decides to impose a penalty on a person under section 63A, the person may refer the matter to the Tribunal.

63C Statement of policy

(1) The Authority must prepare and issue a statement of its policy with respect to —
  (a) the imposition of penalties under section 63A; and
  (b) the amount of penalties under that section.

(2) The Authority's policy in determining whether a penalty should be imposed, and what the amount of a penalty should be, must include having regard to —
  (a) the conduct of the person on whom the penalty is to be imposed;

(b) the extent to which the person could reasonably be expected to have known that a controlled function was performed without approval;

(c) the length of the period during which the person performed a controlled function without approval; and

(d) whether the person on whom the penalty is to be imposed is an individual.

(3) The Authority's policy in determining whether a penalty should be imposed on a person must also include having regard to the appropriateness of taking action against the person instead of, or in addition to, taking action against an authorised person.

(4) A statement issued under this section must include an indication of the circumstances in which the Authority would expect to be satisfied that a person could reasonably be expected to have known that the person was performing a controlled function without approval.

(5) The Authority may at any time alter or replace a statement issued under this section.

(6) If a statement issued under this section is altered or replaced, the Authority must issue the altered or replaced statement.

(7) The Authority must, without delay, give the Treasury a copy of any statement which it publishes under this section.

(8) A statement issued under this section must be published by the Authority in the way appearing to the Authority to be best calculated to bring it to the attention of the public.

(9) The Authority may charge a reasonable fee for providing a person with a copy of the statement.

(10) In exercising, or deciding whether to exercise, its power under section 63A in the case of any particular person, the Authority must have regard to any statement of policy published under this section and in force at a time when the person concerned performed a controlled function without approval.

63D Statement of policy: procedure

(1) Before issuing a statement under section 63C, the Authority must publish a draft of the proposed statement in the way appearing to the Authority to be best calculated to bring it to the attention of the public.

(2) The draft must be accompanied by notice that representations about the proposal may be made to the Authority within a specified time.

(3) Before issuing the proposed statement, the Authority must have regard to any representations made to it in accordance with subsection (2).

(4) If the Authority issues the proposed statement it must publish an account, in general terms, of—

(a) the representations made to it in accordance with subsection (2); and

(b) its response to them.

(5) If the statement differs from the draft published under subsection (1) in a way which is, in the opinion of the Authority, significant, the Authority must (in addition to complying with subsection (4)) publish details of the difference.

(6) The Authority may charge a reasonable fee for providing a person with a copy of a draft published under subsection (1).

(7) This section also applies to a proposal to alter or replace a statement."

12 Approved persons guilty of misconduct

(1) Section 66 of the Financial Services and Markets Act 2000 (performance of regulated activities: disciplinary powers) is amended as follows.

(2) In subsection (3) —
   (a) in the opening words, for "it may — " substitute "it may do one or more of the following — ", and
   (b) after paragraph (a) (but before the "or" at the end of it) insert —
      "(aa) suspend, for such period as it considers appropriate, any approval of the performance by him of any function to which the approval relates;
      (ab) impose, for such period as it considers appropriate, such limitations or other restrictions in relation to the performance by him of any function to which any approval relates as it considers appropriate;".

(3) After that subsection insert —

   "(3A) The period for which a suspension or restriction is to have effect may not exceed two years.

   (3B) A suspension or restriction may have effect in relation to part of a function.

   (3C) A restriction may, in particular, be imposed so as to require any person to take, or refrain from taking, specified action.

   (3D) The Authority may —
      (a) withdraw a suspension or restriction; or
      (b) vary a suspension or restriction so as to reduce the period for which it has effect or otherwise to limit its effect."

(4) In subsection (4), for "two years" substitute "three years".

13 Publication of decision notices

(1) Section 391 of the Financial Services and Markets Act 2000 (publication) is amended as follows.

(2) In subsection (1) (which prevents the FSA and the person to whom a warning or decision notice is given or copied from publishing the notice or any details concerning it), omit "or decision notice".

(3) After that subsection insert—

"(1A) A person to whom a decision notice is given or copied may not publish the notice or any details concerning it unless the Authority has published the notice or those details."

(4) In subsection (4) (duty of FSA to publish information about a final notice), before "final notice" insert "decision notice or".

Measures to protect consumers

14 Consumer redress schemes

(1) In the Financial Services and Markets Act 2000, for section 404 (and the italic cross-heading before it) substitute—

"Consumer redress schemes

404 Consumer redress schemes

(1) This section applies if—
  (a) it appears to the Authority that there may have been a widespread or regular failure by relevant firms to comply with requirements applicable to the carrying on by them of any activity;
  (b) it appears to it that, as a result, consumers have suffered (or may suffer) loss or damage in respect of which, if they brought legal proceedings, a remedy or relief would be available in the proceedings; and
  (c) it considers that it is desirable to make rules for the purpose of securing that redress is made to the consumers in respect of the failure (having regard to other ways in which consumers may obtain redress).

(2) "Relevant firms" means—
  (a) authorised persons; or
  (b) payment service providers.

(3) The Authority may make rules requiring each relevant firm (or each relevant firm of a specified description) which has carried on the activity on or after the specified date to establish and operate a consumer redress scheme.

(4) A "consumer redress scheme" is a scheme under which the firm is required to take one or more of the following steps in relation to the activity.

(5) The firm must first investigate whether, on or after the specified date, it has failed to comply with the requirements mentioned in subsection (1)(a) that are applicable to the carrying on by it of the activity.

(6) The next step is for the firm to determine whether the failure has caused (or may cause) loss or damage to consumers.

(7) If the firm determines that the failure has caused (or may cause) loss or damage to consumers, it must then—

(a) determine what the redress should be in respect of the failure; and

(b) make the redress to the consumers.

(8) A relevant firm is required to take the above steps in relation to any particular consumer even if, after the rules are made, a defence of limitation becomes available to the firm in respect of the loss or damage in question.

(9) Before making rules under this section, the Authority must consult the scheme operator of the ombudsman scheme.

(10) For the meaning of consumers, see section 404E.

404A Rules under s.404: supplementary

(1) Rules under section 404 may make provision—

(a) specifying the activities and requirements in relation to which relevant firms are to carry out investigations under consumer redress schemes;

(b) setting out, in relation to any specified description of case, examples of things done, or omitted to be done, that are to be regarded as constituting a failure to comply with a requirement;

(c) setting out, in relation to any specified description of case, matters to be taken into account, or steps to be taken, by relevant firms for the purpose of—

(i) assessing evidence as to a failure to comply with a requirement; or

(ii) determining whether such a failure has caused (or may cause) loss or damage to consumers;

(d) as to the kinds of redress that are, or are not, to be made to consumers in specified descriptions of case and the way in which redress is to be determined in specified descriptions of case;

(e) as to the things that relevant firms are, or are not, to do in establishing and operating consumer redress schemes;

(f) securing that relevant firms are not required to investigate anything occurring after a specified date;

(g) specifying the times by which anything required to be done under any consumer redress scheme is to be done;

(h) requiring relevant firms to provide information to the Authority;

(i) authorising one or more competent persons to do anything for the purposes of, or in connection with, the establishment or operation of any consumer redress scheme;

(j) for the nomination or approval by the Authority of persons authorised under paragraph (i);

(k) as to the circumstances in which, instead of a relevant firm, the Authority (or one or more competent persons acting on the Authority's behalf) may carry out the investigation and take the other relevant steps under any consumer redress scheme;

(l) as to the powers to be available to those carrying out an investigation by virtue of paragraph (k);

(m) as to the enforcement of any redress (for example, in the case of a money award, as a debt owed by a relevant firm).

(2) The only examples that may be set out in the rules as a result of subsection (1)(b) are examples of things done, or omitted to be done, that have been, or would be, held by a court or tribunal to constitute a failure to comply with a requirement.

(3) Matters may not be set out in the rules as a result of subsection (1)(c) if they have not been, or would not be, taken into account by a court or tribunal for the purpose mentioned there.

(4) The Authority must exercise the power conferred as a result of subsection (1)(d) so as to secure that, in relation to any description of case, the only kinds of redress to be made are those which it considers to be just in relation to that description of case.

(5) In acting under subsection (4), the Authority must have regard (among other things) to the nature and extent of the losses or damage in question.

(6) The provision that may be made under subsection (1)(h) includes provision applying (with or without modifications) —
    (a) any provision of section 165; or
    (b) any provision of Part 11 relating to that section.

(7) The reference in subsection (1)(k) to the other relevant steps under any consumer redress scheme is a reference to the Authority making the determinations mentioned in section 404(6) and (7) (with the firm still required to make the redress).

(8) If the rules include provision under subsection (1)(k), they must also include provision for —
    (a) giving warning and decision notices, and
    (b) conferring rights on relevant firms to refer matters to the Tribunal,
in relation to any determination mentioned in section 404(6) and (7) made by the Authority.

(9) Nothing in this section is to be taken as limiting the power conferred by section 404.

404B Complaints to the ombudsman scheme

(1) If —
    (a) a consumer makes a complaint under the ombudsman scheme in respect of an act or omission of a relevant firm, and
    (b) at the time the complaint is made, the subject-matter of the complaint falls to be dealt with (or has been dealt with) under a consumer redress scheme,
the way in which the complaint is to be determined by the ombudsman is to be as mentioned in subsection (4).

(2) If a consumer —
    (a) is not satisfied with a determination made by a relevant firm under a consumer redress scheme, or

(b) considers that a relevant firm has failed to make a determination in accordance with a consumer redress scheme,

the consumer may, in respect of that determination or failure, make a complaint under the ombudsman scheme.

(3) A complaint mentioned in subsection (1) or (2) is referred to in the following provisions of this section as a "relevant complaint".

(4) A relevant complaint is to be determined by reference to what, in the opinion of the ombudsman, the determination under the consumer redress scheme should be or should have been (subject to subsection (5)).

(5) If, in determining a relevant complaint, the ombudsman determines that the firm should make (or should have made) a payment of an amount to the consumer, the amount awarded by the ombudsman (a "money award") must not exceed the monetary limit (within the meaning of section 229).

(6) But the ombudsman may recommend that the firm pay a larger amount.

(7) A money award—
   (a) may specify the date by which the amount awarded is to be paid;
   (b) may provide for interest to be payable, at a rate specified in the award, on any amount which is not paid by that date; and
   (c) is enforceable by the consumer in accordance with Part 3 or 3A of Schedule 17 (as the case may be).

(8) If, in determining a relevant complaint, the ombudsman determines that the firm should take (or should have taken) particular action in relation to the consumer, the ombudsman may direct the firm to take that action.

(9) Compliance with a direction under subsection (8) is enforceable, on the application of the consumer, by an injunction or, in Scotland, by an order for specific performance under section 45 of the Court of Session Act 1988.

(10) In consequence of the provision made by this section, sections 228(2) and 229 do not apply in relation to relevant complaints; but all other provision made by or under Part 16 applies in relation to those complaints.

(11) The compulsory jurisdiction of the ombudsman scheme is to include the jurisdiction resulting from this section.

(12) Nothing in subsection (1) is to be taken as requiring the ombudsman to determine a complaint in any case where (apart from that subsection) the complaint would not fall to be determined (whether as a result of rules made under Schedule 17 or otherwise).

(13) Nothing in subsection (2) is to be taken as conferring an entitlement on a person who, for the purposes of the ombudsman scheme, is not an eligible complainant in relation to the subject-matter of the determination mentioned there.

404C Enforcement

The following provisions —
  (a) Part 14 (disciplinary measures), and
  (b) so much of this Act as relates to any provision of that Part,
(which apply only in relation to authorised persons) are also to apply in relation to relevant firms which are not (or are no longer) authorised persons.

404D Applications to Tribunal to quash rules or provision of rules

(1) Any person may apply to the Tribunal for a review of any rules made under section 404.

(2) The Tribunal may —
  (a) dismiss the application; or
  (b) make an order (a "quashing order") quashing any rules made under section 404 or any provision of those rules.

(3) An application may be made only if permission to make it has first been obtained from the Tribunal.

(4) The Tribunal may grant permission to make an application only if it considers that the applicant has a sufficient interest in the matter to which the application relates.

(5) The general rule is that, in determining an application, the Tribunal is to apply the principles applicable on an application for judicial review.

(6) If (or so far as) an application relates to an example set out in the rules as a result of section 404A(1)(b), the Tribunal may determine whether the example constitutes a failure to comply with the requirement in question.

(7) If (or so far as) an application relates to a matter set out in the rules as a result of section 404A(1)(c), the Tribunal may determine whether the matter should be taken into account as mentioned in that provision.

(8) In the case of an application within subsection (6) or (7), the Tribunal's jurisdiction under that subsection is in addition to its jurisdiction under subsection (5).

(9) A quashing order may be enforced as if it were an order made, on an application for judicial review, by the High Court or, in Scotland, the Court of Session.

(10) The Tribunal may award damages to the applicant if —
  (a) the application includes a claim for damages arising from any matter to which the application relates; and
  (b) the Tribunal is satisfied that an award would have been made by the High Court or, in Scotland, the Court of Session if the claim had been made in an action begun in that court by the applicant when making the application.

(11) An award of damages under subsection (10) may be enforced as if it were an award made by the High Court or, in Scotland, the Court of Session.

(12) In the case of any proceedings under this section, the judge presiding at the proceedings must be —
    (a) a judge of the High Court or the Court of Appeal or a judge of the Court of Session; or
    (b) such other person as may be agreed from time to time by —
        (i) the Lord Chief Justice, the Lord President or the Lord Chief Justice of Northern Ireland (as the case may be); and
        (ii) the Senior President of Tribunals.

(13) Section 133 does not apply in the case of an application under this section, but —
    (a) Tribunal Procedure Rules may make provision for the suspension of rules made under section 404 or of any provision of those rules, pending determination of the application; and
    (b) in the case of an application within subsection (6) or (7), the Tribunal may consider any evidence relating to the application's subject-matter, whether or not it was available at the time the rules were made.

(14) If —
    (a) the Tribunal refuses to grant permission to make an application under this section, and
    (b) on an appeal by the applicant, the Court of Appeal grants the permission,
the Court of Appeal may go on to decide the application under this section.

404E Meaning of "consumers"

(1) For the purposes of sections 404 to 404B "consumers" means persons who —
    (a) have used, or may have contemplated using, any of the services within subsection (2); or
    (b) have relevant rights or interests in relation to any of the services within that subsection.

(2) The services within this subsection are services provided by —
    (a) authorised persons in carrying on regulated activities;
    (b) authorised persons in carrying on a consumer credit business in connection with the accepting of deposits;
    (c) authorised persons in communicating, or approving the communication by others of, invitations or inducements to engage in investment activity;
    (d) authorised persons who are investment firms, or credit institutions, in providing relevant ancillary services;
    (e) persons acting as appointed representatives; or
    (f) payment service providers in providing payment services.

(3) A person ("P") has a "relevant right or interest" in relation to any services within subsection (2) if P has a right or interest —
    (a) which is derived from, or is otherwise attributable to, the use of the services by others; or

(b) which may be adversely affected by the use of the services by persons acting on P's behalf or in a fiduciary capacity in relation to P.

(4) If a person is providing a service within subsection (2) as a trustee, the persons who have been, or may have been, beneficiaries of the trust are to be treated as persons who have used, or may have contemplated using, the service.

(5) A person who deals with another person ("B") in the course of B providing a service within subsection (2) is to be treated as using the service.

(6) In this section—

"accepting", in relation to deposits, includes agreeing to accept;

"consumer credit business" has the same meaning as in the Consumer Credit Act 1974 (see section 189(1));

"credit institution" has the meaning given by section 138(1B);

"engage in investment activity" has the meaning given by section 21;

"payment services" has the same meaning as in the Payment Services Regulations 2009;

"payment service provider" means a person who is a payment service provider for the purposes of those regulations as a result of falling within any of paragraphs (a) to (e) of the definition in regulation 2(1);

"relevant ancillary services" has the meaning given by section 138(1C).

404F Other definitions etc

(1) For the purposes of sections 404 to 404B—

"redress" includes—

(a) interest; and

(b) a remedy or relief which could not be awarded in legal proceedings;

"specified" means specified in rules made under section 404.

(2) In determining for the purposes of those sections whether an authorised person has failed to comply with a requirement, anything which an appointed representative has done or omitted as respects business for which the authorised person has accepted responsibility is to be treated as having been done or omitted by the authorised person.

(3) References in those sections to the failure by a relevant firm to comply with a requirement applicable to the carrying on by it of any activity include anything done, or omitted to be done, by it in carrying on the activity—

(a) which is in breach of a duty or other obligation, prohibition or restriction; or

(b) which otherwise gives rise to the availability of a remedy or relief in legal proceedings.

(4) It does not matter whether—

(a) the duty or other obligation, prohibition or restriction, or

(b) the remedy or relief,

arises as a result of any provision made by or under this or any other Act, a rule of law or otherwise.

(5) References in sections 404 to 404B to a relevant firm include—

(a) a person who was at any time a relevant firm but has subsequently ceased to be one; and

(b) a person who has assumed a liability (including a contingent one) incurred by a relevant firm in respect of a failure by the firm to comply with a requirement applicable to the carrying on by it of any activity.

(6) References in those sections to the carrying on of an activity by a relevant firm are, accordingly, to be read in that case with the appropriate modifications.

(7) If the Authority varies a permission or authorisation of a person so as to impose requirements on the person to establish and operate a scheme which corresponds to, or is similar to, a consumer redress scheme, the provision that may be included in the permission or authorisation as varied includes—

(a) provision imposing requirements on the person corresponding to those that could be included in rules made under section 404; and

(b) provision corresponding to section 404B.

(8) In subsection (7) the reference to the variation of a permission or authorisation by the Authority is a reference to—

(a) the variation under section 44 or 45 of a Part IV permission; or

(b) the variation under regulation 8 or 11 of the Payment Services Regulations 2009 of an authorisation under those regulations.

404G Power to widen the scope of consumer redress schemes

(1) The Treasury may by order amend the definition of "relevant firms" in section 404 or the definition of "consumers" in section 404E (or both).

(2) An order under this section may make consequential amendments of any provision of sections 404 to 404F."

(2) This section has effect in relation to failures occurring before the commencement of this section (as well as in relation to failures occurring at or after the commencement of this section).

15 Restrictions on provision of credit card cheques

(1) The Consumer Credit Act 1974 ("the CCA 1974") is amended as follows.

(2) After section 51 insert—

"51A Restrictions on provision of credit card cheques

(1) A person who provides credit card cheques otherwise than in accordance with this section commits an offence.

(2) Credit card cheques may be provided only to a person who has asked for them.

(3) They may be provided only on a single occasion in respect of each request that is made.

(4) The number of cheques provided in respect of a request must not exceed three (or, if less, the number requested).

(5) Where a single request is made for the provision of credit card cheques in connection with more than one credit-token agreement, subsections (3) and (4) apply as if a separate request had been made in relation to each agreement.

(6) Where more than one request for the provision of cheques is made in the same document or at the same time—
   (a) they may be provided in respect of only one of the requests, but
   (b) if the requests relate to more than one credit-token agreement, in relation to each agreement they may be provided only in respect of one of the requests made in relation to that agreement.

(7) "Credit card cheque" means a cheque (whether or not drawn on a banker) which, whenever used, will result in the provision of credit under a credit-token agreement.

(8) Accordingly, "credit card cheque" does not include a cheque to be used only in connection with a current account.

51B Section 51A: exemption for business

(1) Section 51A does not apply to credit card cheques provided in connection with a credit-token agreement that is entered into by the debtor wholly or predominantly for the purposes of a business carried on, or intended to be carried on, by the debtor.

(2) If a credit-token agreement includes a declaration made by the debtor to the effect that the agreement is entered into as mentioned in subsection (1), the agreement is treated for the purposes of that subsection as having been so entered into.

(3) Subsection (2) does not apply if, when the agreement is entered into—
   (a) the creditor, or
   (b) any person who has acted on behalf of the creditor in connection with the entering into of the agreement,
   knows, or has reasonable cause to suspect, that the agreement is not entered into as mentioned in subsection (1).

(4) The Secretary of State may by order make provision about the form, content and signing of declarations for the purposes of subsection (2).

(5) Where an agreement has two or more creditors, references in subsection (3) to the creditor are to any one or more of them."

(3) In Schedule 1 (prosecution and punishment of offences), after the entry relating to section 51(1) insert—

"51A(1)	Breach of restrictions on provision of credit card cheques.	(a) Summarily.	The statutory maximum.
		(b) On indictment.	A fine."

(4) An offence under section 51A of the CCA 1974 is to be treated for the purposes of Part 3 of the Regulatory Enforcement and Sanctions Act 2008 (civil sanctions) as contained in the CCA 1974 immediately before the day on which that Act of 2008 was passed.

Financial Services Compensation Scheme

16 Contribution to costs of special resolution regime

(1) In the Financial Services and Markets Act 2000, for section 214B substitute—

"**214B Contribution to costs of special resolution regime**

(1) This section applies if—

    (a) a stabilisation power under Part 1 of the Banking Act 2009 has been exercised in respect of a bank, building society or credit union within the meaning of that Part ("the institution"); and

    (b) the Treasury think that the institution was or was likely to have been, or but for the exercise of the power would have become, unable to satisfy claims against it.

(2) The Treasury may require the scheme manager to make payments (to the Treasury or any other person) in respect of expenses of a prescribed description incurred (by the Treasury or that person) in connection with the exercise of the power.

(3) Subsection (2) is subject to section 214C (limit on amount of special resolution regime payments).

(4) In subsection (2) "expenses" includes interest at a specified rate on the difference, at any time, between—

    (a) the total amount of expenses (including interest) incurred at or before that time; and

    (b) the total amount recovered, or received from the scheme manager, in respect of the institution, at or before that time, by—

        (i) the Treasury; and

        (ii) any other person who has incurred expenses in connection with the exercise of the power that are of a description prescribed under subsection (2).

(5) Any payment made by the scheme manager under subsection (2) is to be treated for the purposes of this Part as an expense under the compensation scheme.

(6) In this section and section 214C "specified rate" means a rate specified by the Treasury.

(7) Different rates may be specified under different provisions or for different periods.

(8) A rate may be specified by reference to a rate set (from time to time) by any person.

214C Limit on amount of special resolution regime payments

(1) The total amount of special resolution regime payments required to be made in respect of a person ("the institution") may not exceed —
   (a) notional net expenditure (see subsection (3)), minus
   (b) actual net expenditure (see subsection (4)).

(2) A "special resolution regime payment" is —
   (a) a payment under section 214B(2); or
   (b) a payment required to be made by the scheme manager by virtue of section 61 of the Banking Act 2009 (special resolution regime: compensation).

(3) Notional net expenditure is —
   (a) the total amount of expenses that would have been incurred under the compensation scheme in respect of the institution if the stabilisation power had not been exercised and the institution had been unable to satisfy claims against it, minus
   (b) the total amount that would have been likely, at the time when the power was exercised, to be recovered by the scheme manager in respect of the institution in those circumstances.

(4) Actual net expenditure is —
   (a) the total amount of expenses (other than special resolution regime payments) actually incurred by the scheme manager in respect of the institution, minus
   (b) the total amount actually recovered by the scheme manager in respect of the institution.

(5) In subsection (3)(a) "expenses" includes interest at a specified rate on the difference, at any time, between —
   (a) the total amount of expenses (including interest) that would have been incurred as mentioned in subsection (3)(a) at or before that time; and
   (b) the total amount that would have been likely to have been recovered as mentioned in subsection (3)(b) at or before that time.

(6) In subsection (4)(a) "expenses" includes interest at a specified rate on the difference, at any time, between —
   (a) the total amount of expenses (including special resolution regime payments and interest) actually incurred by the scheme manager in respect of the institution at or before that time; and
   (b) the total amount actually recovered by the scheme manager in respect of the institution at or before that time.

(7) In paragraph (b) of subsections (3) to (6) references to amounts recovered (or likely to have been recovered) by the scheme manager do not include any levy received (or likely to have been received) by it.

214D Contributions under section 214B: supplementary

(1) This section supplements sections 214B and 214C.

(2) The scheme manager must determine —

(a) the amounts of expenses (other than interest) that would have been incurred as mentioned in section 214C(3)(a); and

(b) the time or times at which those amounts would have been likely to have been incurred.

(3) The Treasury, or a person designated by the Treasury, must in accordance with regulations appoint a person ("the valuer") to determine —

(a) the amounts that would have been likely, at the time when the stabilisation power was exercised, to be recovered as mentioned in section 214C(3)(b); and

(b) the time or times at which those amounts would have been likely to be recovered.

The person appointed under this subsection may be the person appointed as valuer under section 54 of the Banking Act 2009 in respect of the exercise of the stabilisation power.

(4) Regulations may enable the Treasury to specify principles to be applied by —

(a) the scheme manager when exercising functions under subsection (2); or

(b) the valuer when exercising functions under subsection (3).

(5) The regulations may in particular enable the Treasury to require the scheme manager or valuer —

(a) to use, or not to use, specified methods;

(b) to take specified matters into account in a specified manner; or

(c) not to take specified matters into account.

(6) Regulations —

(a) must provide for independent verification of expenses within section 214B(2);

(b) may provide for the independent verification of other matters; and

(c) may contain provision about the appointment and payment of an auditor.

(7) Regulations —

(a) must contain provision enabling the valuer to reconsider a decision;

(b) must provide a right of appeal to a court or tribunal against any decision of the valuer;

(c) may provide for payment of the valuer; and

(d) may apply (with or without modifications) or make provision corresponding to —

(i) any provision of sections 54 to 56 of the Banking Act 2009; or

(ii) any provision made, or that could be made, by virtue of any of those sections.

(8) Regulations may make provision for payments under section 214B(2) to be made —

(a) before any verification required by the regulations is undertaken, and

(b) before the limit imposed by section 214C is calculated, subject to any necessary later adjustment.

(9) If they do so they must provide that the amount of any payment required by virtue of subsection (8) must not be such as to give rise to an expectation that an amount will be required to be repaid to the scheme manager (once any necessary verification has been undertaken and the limit imposed by section 214C has been calculated).

(10) Regulations may —
   (a) make provision supplementing section 214B or 214C or this section;
   (b) make further provision about the method by which amounts to be paid under section 214B(2) are to be determined;
   (c) make provision about timing;
   (d) make provision about procedures to be followed;
   (e) provide for discretionary functions to be exercised by a specified body or by persons of a specified class; and
   (f) make provision about the resolution of disputes (which may include provision conferring jurisdiction on a court or tribunal).

(11) "Regulations" means regulations made by the Treasury.

(12) Any payment made by the Treasury by virtue of this section is to be met out of money provided by Parliament.

(13) The compensation scheme may make provision about payments under section 214B(2) and levies in connection with such payments (except provision inconsistent with any provision made by or under section 214B or 214C or this section)."

(2) Sections 214B to 214D of the Financial Services and Markets Act 2000 (as substituted by subsection (1)) apply to any case where a stabilisation power was exercised before the commencement of this section as if the references in sections 214B(4) and 214C(5) and (6) of that Act to any time were to any time on or after 19 November 2009.

17 Power to require FSCS manager to act in relation to other schemes

In the Financial Services and Markets Act 2000, after Part 15 insert —

"PART 15A

POWER TO REQUIRE FSCS MANAGER TO ACT IN RELATION TO OTHER SCHEMES

Introduction

224B Meaning of "relevant scheme" etc

(1) The following provisions apply for the purposes of this Part.

(2) "Relevant scheme" means a scheme or arrangement (other than the FSCS) for the payment of compensation (in certain cases) to customers of persons who provide financial services or carry on a business connected with the provision of such services.

(3) References to the manager of a relevant scheme are to the person who administers it or (if there is no such person) the person responsible for making payments under it.

(4) "The FSCS" means the Financial Services Compensation Scheme (see section 213(2)).

(5) "The FSCS manager" means the scheme manager as defined by section 212(1).

(6) "Expense" includes anything that, if incurred in relation to the FSCS, would amount to an expense for the purposes of the FSCS.

(7) "Notice" means a notice in writing.

(8) In subsection (2) —
   (a) "customers" includes customers outside the United Kingdom;
   (b) "persons" includes persons outside the United Kingdom;
   (c) references to the provision of financial services include the provision outside the United Kingdom of such services.

(9) This Part applies to cases where the manager of the relevant scheme is the Treasury or any other Minister of the Crown as it applies to cases where that manager is any other person.

Power to require FSCS manager to act

224C Power to require FSCS manager to act on behalf of manager of relevant scheme

(1) This section applies if compensation is payable under a relevant scheme.

(2) The Treasury may by notice require the FSCS manager to exercise (on behalf of the manager of the relevant scheme) specified functions in respect of specified claims for compensation under the relevant scheme.

(3) A notice may be given only with the consent of the manager of the relevant scheme.

(4) In subsection (2) "specified" means specified, or of a description specified, in the notice.

(5) Claims or descriptions of claims may be specified by reference to the persons or description of persons whose claims they are.

224D Cases where FSCS manager may decline to act

(1) This section applies where a notice under section 224C(2) (a "section 224C notice") has been given in respect of a relevant scheme.

(2) The FSCS manager is not under a duty to comply with the section 224C notice if, as soon as reasonably practicable after receiving it, the FSCS manager gives a notice to the Treasury stating that a ground set out in section 224E applies.

(3) Where a notice under subsection (2) is given, the FSCS manager may recover from the manager of the relevant scheme an amount equal to

the total expenses incurred by the FSCS manager in connection with the relevant scheme in the period —
  (a) beginning with the giving of the section 224C notice; and
  (b) ending with the giving of the notice under subsection (2).

(4) The duty to comply with the section 224C notice ceases if, after starting to comply with it, the FSCS manager gives a notice to the Treasury and the manager of the relevant scheme stating that a ground set out in section 224E applies.

(5) Where a notice under subsection (4) is given, the FSCS manager must give the Treasury such information connected with the FSCS manager's exercise of functions in relation to the relevant scheme as the Treasury may reasonably require.

(6) Any notice under this section —
  (a) may be given only if, before giving it, the FSCS manager has taken reasonable steps to deal with anything that is causing the ground or grounds in question to apply; and
  (b) must contain details of those steps.

224E Grounds for declining to act

(1) This section sets out the grounds referred to in section 224D(2) and (4).

(2) The first ground is that the FSCS manager is not satisfied that it will be able to obtain any information required in order to comply with the section 224C notice.

(3) The second ground is that the FSCS manager is not satisfied that it will be able to obtain any advice or other assistance from the manager of the relevant scheme that is required in order to comply with the section 224C notice.

(4) The third ground is —
  (a) that the FSCS manager has not received an amount at least equal to the total expenses it expects to incur in connection with its relevant scheme functions; and
  (b) either —
    (i) that there are no arrangements for the provision of funds to the FSCS manager to enable it to exercise those functions and meet those expenses; or
    (ii) that the FSCS manager considers that any such arrangements are unsatisfactory.

(5) The fourth ground is that the FSCS manager considers that complying with the section 224C notice would detrimentally affect the exercise of its functions under the FSCS.

(6) The fifth ground is —
  (a) that there is no undertaking from the manager of the relevant scheme not to bring proceedings against the FSCS manager; or
  (b) that the FSCS manager considers that the terms of any such undertaking are unsatisfactory.

(7) The sixth ground is —

(a) that there are no arrangements for the reimbursement of any expenses incurred by the FSCS manager in connection with any proceedings brought against it in respect of its relevant scheme functions (including expenses incurred in meeting any award of damages made against it); or

(b) that the FSCS manager considers that any such arrangements are unsatisfactory.

(8) In subsection (6) references to an undertaking of the kind mentioned there are to an undertaking not to bring proceedings in respect of the FSCS manager's relevant scheme functions except proceedings in respect of an act or omission of the FSCS manager that is alleged to have been in bad faith.

(9) In this section "proceedings" includes proceedings outside the United Kingdom.

Rules

224F Rules about relevant schemes

(1) The Authority may by rules make provision in connection with the exercise by the FSCS manager of functions in respect of relevant schemes.

(2) The provision that may be made by the rules includes any provision corresponding to provision that could be contained in the FSCS; but this is subject to subsections (3) and (4).

(3) The rules may confer on the FSCS manager a power to impose levies on authorised persons (or any class of authorised persons) for the purpose of meeting its management expenses incurred in connection with its functions in respect of relevant schemes.

(4) But if the rules confer such a power they must provide that the power may be exercised in relation to expenses incurred in connection with a relevant scheme only if the FSCS manager has tried its best to obtain reimbursement of the expenses from the manager of the relevant scheme.

(5) The rules may apply any provision of the FSCS, with or without modifications.

(6) An amount payable to the FSCS manager as a result of any provision of the rules made by virtue of subsection (3) may be recovered as a debt due to the FSCS manager.

(7) References to the FSCS manager's "management expenses" are to its expenses incurred otherwise than in paying compensation."

Powers to require information

18 Information relating to financial stability

(1) The Financial Services and Markets Act 2000 is amended as follows.

(2) After section 165 insert—

"**165A Authority's power to require information: financial stability**

(1) The Authority may, by notice in writing given to a person to whom this section applies, require the person—
   (a) to provide specified information or information of a specified description; or
   (b) to produce specified documents or documents of a specified description.

(2) This section applies to—
   (a) a person who has a legal or beneficial interest in any of the assets of a relevant investment fund;
   (b) a person who is responsible for the management of a relevant investment fund;
   (c) a person (a "service provider") who provides any service to an authorised person;
   (d) a person prescribed by an order made by the Treasury or any person of a description prescribed by such an order (and see also section 165C);
   (e) a person who is connected with a person to whom this section applies as a result of any of the above paragraphs.

(3) This section applies only to information and documents that the Authority considers are, or might be, relevant to the stability of one or more aspects of the UK financial system.

(4) A notice may be given to a service provider, or to a person who is connected with a service provider, only if the Authority considers that—
   (a) the service or the way in which it (or any part of it) is provided, or
   (b) any failure to provide the service (or any part of it),
   poses, or would be likely to pose, a serious threat to the stability of the UK financial system.

(5) Information or documents required under this section must be provided or produced—
   (a) before the end of such reasonable period as may be specified; and
   (b) at such place as may be specified.

(6) The Authority may require any information provided under this section to be provided in such form as it may reasonably require.

(7) The Authority may require—
   (a) any information provided, whether in a document or otherwise, to be verified in such manner as it may reasonably require; or
   (b) any document produced to be authenticated in such manner as it may reasonably require.

(8) In this section—
   "management" includes any of the activities listed in Annex II to the UCITS directive;

"relevant investment fund" means an investment fund whose assets consist of or include financial instruments which —
(a) are traded in the United Kingdom; or
(b) were issued by a body incorporated in the United Kingdom;

"service" includes facility;

"specified" means specified in the notice.

(9) For the purposes of the definition of "relevant investment fund" —
(a) arrangements may constitute an investment fund even if there is only one person participating in the arrangements; and
(b) the reference to financial instruments has the meaning given by Article 4.1(17) of the markets in financial instruments directive.

(10) For the purposes of this section a person is connected with another person ("A") if the person is or has at any relevant time been —
(a) a member of A's group;
(b) a controller of A;
(c) any other member of a partnership of which A is a member; or
(d) in relation to A, a person mentioned in Part 1 of Schedule 15 (reading references in that Part to the authorised person as references to A).

165B Safeguards etc in relation to exercise of power under section 165A

(1) If the Authority proposes to impose a requirement on a person under section 165A, it must give the person a notice in writing warning the person that the Authority is proposing to impose the requirement.

(2) The notice under subsection (1) must —
(a) give the Authority's reasons for proposing to impose the requirement; and
(b) specify a reasonable period within which the person may make representations to the Authority.

(3) The Authority must then decide, within a reasonable period, whether to impose the requirement.

(4) Subsections (1) to (3) do not apply in any case where the Authority is satisfied that it is necessary for the information or documents to be provided or produced without delay.

(5) If the Authority imposes a requirement on a person under section 165A, the notice under that section must give the Authority's reasons for imposing the requirement.

(6) The Authority must prepare a statement of its policy with respect to the exercise of the power conferred by section 165A.

(7) The statement requires the approval of the Treasury.

(8) If the Treasury approve the statement, the Authority must publish it.

(9) The power conferred by section 165A may not be exercised before the statement has been published.

165C Orders under section 165A(2)(d)

(1) The Treasury may make an order under section 165A(2)(d) only if they consider that —

    (a) the activities carried on by the prescribed person or persons of the prescribed description, or the way in which those activities (or any part of them) are carried on, or

    (b) any failure to carry on those activities (or any part of them),

pose, or would be likely to pose, a serious threat to the stability of the UK financial system.

(2) Subject as follows, an order under section 165A(2)(d) may not be made unless a draft of the order has been laid before, and approved by a resolution of, each House of Parliament.

(3) Subsection (2) does not apply in any case where the Treasury are satisfied that it is necessary to make an order under section 165A(2)(d) without laying a draft for approval.

(4) In that case, the order —

    (a) must be laid before Parliament after being made; and

    (b) ceases to have effect at the end of the relevant period unless before the end of that period it is approved by a resolution of each House of Parliament.

(5) If an order ceases to have effect as a result of subsection (4)(b) that does not affect —

    (a) anything done under it; or

    (b) the power to make a new one.

(6) "Relevant period" means a period of 28 days beginning with the day on which the order is made.

(7) In calculating the relevant period no account is to be taken of any time during which Parliament is dissolved or prorogued or during which both Houses are adjourned for more than four days.

(8) If a statutory instrument containing an order under section 165A(2)(d) would, apart from this subsection, be treated as a hybrid instrument for the purposes of the Standing Orders of either House of Parliament, it is to proceed in that House as if it were not a hybrid instrument."

(3) After section 169 insert —

"169A Support of overseas regulator with respect to financial stability

(1) At the request of an overseas regulator, the Authority may exercise a corresponding section 165A power.

(2) An "overseas regulator" means an authority in a country or territory outside the United Kingdom which exercises functions with respect to the stability of the financial system operating in that country or territory.

(3) A "corresponding section 165A power" means a power corresponding to the one conferred by section 165A, but reading references in that section to the stability of the UK financial system as references to the

stability of the financial system operating in the country or territory of the overseas regulator.

(4) The following provisions apply in relation to the exercise of the corresponding section 165A power—
   (a) section 165B(1) to (5); and
   (b) section 169(3), (4)(a) and (d), (5) and (6).

(5) In this section "the financial system" includes—
   (a) financial markets and exchanges;
   (b) activities that would be regulated activities if carried on in the United Kingdom; and
   (c) other activities connected with financial markets and exchanges."

19 Asset protection scheme etc

(1) The Treasury may, by notice in writing, require a person who participates (or is proposing to participate) in the asset protection scheme or a qualifying scheme—
   (a) to provide such information, or
   (b) to produce such documents,
   as they may reasonably require for the purposes of, or in connection with, the scheme or a relevant scheme agreement.

(2) "The asset protection scheme" means the scheme known as the Asset Protection Scheme that was the subject of a statement made by the Chancellor of the Exchequer on 26 February 2009.

(3) "Qualifying scheme" means a scheme specified in an order made by the Treasury.

(4) "Relevant scheme agreement" means an agreement entered into (or proposed to be entered into) under the asset protection scheme or a qualifying scheme.

(5) The information or documents must be provided or produced at such times, and at such place, as the Treasury may specify in the notice.

(6) The Treasury may require the information to be provided in such form as they may reasonably require.

(7) A requirement imposed on a person as a result of this section is enforceable by an injunction or, in Scotland, by an order for specific performance under section 45 of the Court of Session Act 1988.

(8) The Treasury may specify a scheme in an order under subsection (3) only if it appears to them that the purpose of the scheme corresponds to, or is connected with, the purpose of the asset protection scheme.

(9) An order under subsection (3) is subject to negative resolution procedure.

Banking Act 2009

20 Services forming part of recognised inter-bank payment systems

In Part 5 of the Banking Act 2009 (inter-bank payment systems), after section

206 insert—

"206A Services forming part of recognised inter-bank payment systems

(1) The Treasury may by order make provision applying any provision of this Part to persons who are service providers in relation to a recognised inter-bank payment system.

(2) A person is a service provider in relation to a recognised inter-bank payment system if—
    (a) the person provides services that form part of the arrangements constituting the system, and
    (b) the person is specified as a person within paragraph (a) by the Treasury in the recognition order made in respect of the system.

(3) Telecommunication or information technology services are examples of the kind of services that may fall within subsection (2)(a).

(4) Before specifying persons under subsection (2)(b), the Treasury must—
    (a) consult the Bank of England and the FSA,
    (b) notify the operator of the system and the persons whom the Treasury proposes to specify, and
    (c) consider any representations made.

(5) The Treasury may not specify the Bank of England under subsection (2)(b).

(6) Before making an order under subsection (1), the Treasury must consult—
    (a) the Bank of England,
    (b) the FSA, and
    (c) such other persons as the Treasury consider appropriate.

(7) An order under subsection (1)—
    (a) may modify any provision of this Part in its application to persons who are service providers in relation to a recognised inter-bank payment system;
    (b) may (but need not) take the form of textual amendment.

(8) An order under subsection (1)—
    (a) is to be made by statutory instrument, and
    (b) may not be made unless a draft has been laid before and approved by resolution of each House of Parliament."

21 Minor amendments of provision made by Banking Act 2009

(1) The Banking Act 2009 is amended as follows.

(2) After section 48 insert—

"48A Creation of liabilities

(1) The provision that may be made by a property transfer instrument or order in reliance on section 33(1)(b), 42(3)(b), 43(3)(b), 44(4)(c), 45(3)(b) or 46(3)(b) includes provision for the creation of liabilities.

(2) The provision may be framed by reference to an agreement which has been or is to be entered into, or anything else which has been or is to be done, by any person (including a person other than the person making the instrument or order)."

(3) In section 55 (independent valuer: supplemental), at the end insert—

"(10) But subsection (9)(b) does not apply if the order is contained in a statutory instrument that contains an order to which section 62 applies."

(4) In section 56 (independent valuer: money)—

(a) in subsection (1), after paragraph (c) (but before the "and" at the end of it) insert—

"(ca) persons mentioned in section 54(4)(b),", and

(b) at the end insert—

"(6) But subsection (5)(b) does not apply if the order is contained in a statutory instrument that contains an order to which section 62 applies."

(5) In section 84 (application of Part 1 to building societies), in the entry in the table relating to sections 49 to 62, in paragraph (c) of the third column, at the end insert "but the Treasury may make a third party compensation order".

(6) In section 145(6) (bank administration: general powers, duties and effect), in table 1 of applied provisions (Schedule B1 to the Insolvency Act 1986), for the entry relating to paragraph 80 substitute—

"Para. 79	Termination: successful rescue	(a) Ignore sub-para. (2). (b) See section 153."

(7) In section 153 (successful rescue), for subsections (2) and (3) substitute—

"(2) The bank administrator shall make an application under paragraph 79 of Schedule B1 to the Insolvency Act 1986 (court ending administration on achievement of objectives).

(3) A bank administrator who makes an application in accordance with subsection (2) must send a copy to the FSA."

(8) In section 219(3A) of the Financial Services and Markets Act 2000 (which was inserted by section 176(6) of the Banking Act 2009)—

(a) after "a bank," insert "building society or credit union,", and

(b) for "the bank or the Bank of England" substitute "the bank, building society or credit union, or the Bank of England,".

Director of Savings

22 Administration of court funds by Director of Savings

(1) In this section "relevant function" means a function of the Accountant General of the Senior Courts ("the Accountant General") under court funds rules.

(2) The Director of Savings ("the Director") may discharge a relevant function if appointed by the Accountant General under court funds rules to do so.

(3) The functions of the Director that are within section 69(1)(a) of the Deregulation and Contracting Out Act 1994 (contracting out of statutory functions) include any power of the Director, conferred under court funds rules, to discharge a relevant function.

(4) In this section "court funds rules" means rules under section 38(7) of the Administration of Justice Act 1982.

General

23 Orders or regulations

(1) This section applies to orders or regulations under this Act made by the Treasury or the Secretary of State.

(2) Orders or regulations —
 (a) may contain incidental, supplementary, consequential, transitory, transitional or saving provision, and
 (b) may make different provision for different cases or circumstances.

(3) Orders or regulations are to be made by statutory instrument.

(4) Where orders or regulations are subject to "affirmative resolution procedure" the orders or regulations may not be made unless a draft of the statutory instrument containing them has been laid before, and approved by a resolution of, each House of Parliament.

(5) Where orders or regulations are subject to "negative resolution procedure" the statutory instrument containing them is subject to annulment in pursuance of a resolution of either House of Parliament.

24 Minor and consequential amendments

(1) Schedule 2 contains minor and consequential amendments.

(2) In that Schedule —
 Part 1 contains amendments of the Financial Services and Markets Act 2000, and
 Part 2 contains amendments of other legislation.

(3) The Treasury or the Secretary of State may by order make such other provision amending, repealing or revoking any enactment as they consider necessary or expedient in consequence of any provision made by this Act.

(4) "Enactment" includes —
 (a) an enactment contained in subordinate legislation within the meaning of the Interpretation Act 1978,
 (b) an enactment contained in, or in an instrument made under, an Act of the Scottish Parliament,
 (c) an enactment contained in, or in an instrument made under, Northern Ireland legislation, or
 (d) an enactment contained in, or in an instrument made under, a Measure or Act of the National Assembly for Wales.

(5) An order under subsection (3) is subject to negative resolution procedure.

25 Extent

This Act extends to England and Wales, Scotland and Northern Ireland.

26 Commencement

(1) The following provisions of this Act come into force on the day on which this Act is passed—
   (a) section 1,
   (b) section 2(1) and (5) to (8) (subject, in the case of subsection (6), to the exception mentioned in paragraph (k)),
   (c) section 3(1) and (4),
   (d) sections 4 and 5,
   (e) section 16,
   (f) sections 19 to 23,
   (g) in section 24—
       (i) subsections (1) and (2) so far as relating to the paragraphs of Schedule 2 mentioned in paragraph (l), and
       (ii) subsections (3) to (5),
   (h) section 25,
   (i) this section,
   (j) section 27,
   (k) Schedule 1 except so far as that Schedule relates to paragraph 13, 15 or 16 of Schedule 1A to the Financial Services and Markets Act 2000, and
   (l) paragraphs 1 to 6, 11, 13, 16(1) and (2), 22, 24(1) and (2), 25, 27, 28, 30 to 32, 33(1) and (3), 34, 35, 37 to 45 and 48 of Schedule 2.

(2) The following provisions of this Act come into force at the end of the period of 2 months beginning with the day on which this Act is passed—
   (a) section 3(2), (3) and (5),
   (b) sections 6 to 12,
   (c) section 18,
   (d) section 24(1) and (2) so far as relating to the paragraphs of Schedule 2 mentioned in paragraph (e), and
   (e) paragraphs 7 to 10, 12, 14, 15, 16(3), 17 to 20, 26, 29, 33(4), 46 and 47 of Schedule 2.

(3) The other provisions of this Act come into force on such day as the Treasury or the Secretary of State may by order appoint (and different days may be appointed for different purposes).

(4) The Treasury or the Secretary of State may by order make such provision as they consider necessary or expedient for transitory, transitional or saving purposes in connection with the commencement of any provision made by this Act.

27 Short title

This Act may be cited as the Financial Services Act 2010.

SCHEDULES

SCHEDULE 1
Section 2

FURTHER PROVISION ABOUT THE CONSUMER FINANCIAL EDUCATION BODY

1   This is the Schedule 1A to be inserted in the Financial Services and Markets Act 2000 after Schedule 1—

"SCHEDULE 1A
Section 6A

FURTHER PROVISION ABOUT THE CONSUMER FINANCIAL EDUCATION BODY

PART 1

GENERAL

Ensuring exercise of consumer financial education function etc

1   (1) The Authority must take such steps as are necessary to ensure that the consumer financial education body is, at all times, capable of exercising the consumer financial education function.

(2) In complying with the duty under sub-paragraph (1) the Authority may, in particular, provide services to that body which the Authority considers would facilitate the exercise of that function.

Constitution

2   (1) The constitution of the consumer financial education body must provide for it to have—
   (a) a chair;
   (b) a chief executive; and
   (c) a board (which must include the chair and chief executive) whose members are the body's directors.

(2) The members of the board must be persons appointed, and liable to removal from office, by the Authority (acting, in the case of the chair or chief executive, with the approval of the Treasury).

(3) But the terms of appointment of members of the board (and in particular those governing removal from office) must be such as to secure their independence from the Authority in the exercise of the consumer financial education function.

(4) The Authority may appoint a person to be a member of the board only if it is satisfied that the person has knowledge or experience

which is likely to be relevant to the exercise by the body of the consumer financial education function.

Status

3   (1) The consumer financial education body is not to be regarded as exercising functions on behalf of the Crown.

(2) The body's board members, officers and staff are not to be regarded as Crown servants.

Discharge of function by others

4   (1) The consumer financial education body may discharge the consumer financial education function by —
   (a) supporting the doing by other persons of anything that it considers would enhance the understanding, knowledge or ability mentioned in section 6A(1); or
   (b) arranging for other persons to do anything that it considers would enhance that understanding, knowledge or ability.

(2) The reference in sub-paragraph (1)(a) to support includes financial support.

(3) The reference in sub-paragraph (1)(b) to arrangements includes arrangements under which payments are made to the other persons.

(4) Nothing in this paragraph is to limit other ways in which the consumer financial education body may discharge the consumer financial education function.

5   (1) This paragraph applies if the consumer financial education body arranges for any person (including one established by or under an enactment) to do anything that it considers would enhance the understanding, knowledge or ability mentioned in section 6A(1).

(2) The person may do that thing despite any limitation on its capacity (whether under a rule of law or otherwise) which, but for this paragraph, would have applied.

Market confidence and financial stability

6   In discharging the consumer financial education function, the consumer financial education body must have regard to the importance of —
   (a) maintaining confidence in the UK financial system; and
   (b) maintaining the stability of the UK financial system.

Budget

7   (1) The consumer financial education body must adopt an annual budget which has been approved by the Authority.

(2) The budget must be adopted —
   (a) in the case of the body's first financial year, as soon as reasonably practicable after the body is established; and

(b) in the case of each subsequent financial year, before the start of the financial year.

(3) The consumer financial education body may, with the approval of the Authority, vary the budget for a financial year at any time after its adoption.

(4) Before adopting or varying a budget, the consumer financial education body must consult —
  (a) the Treasury;
  (b) the Secretary of State;
  (c) the Office of Fair Trading; and
  (d) such other persons (if any) as the body considers appropriate.

(5) The consumer financial education body must publish each budget, and each variation of a budget, in the way it considers appropriate.

Annual plan

8   (1) The consumer financial education body must in respect of each of its financial years prepare an annual plan which has been approved by the Authority.

(2) The plan must be prepared —
  (a) in the case of the body's first financial year, as soon as reasonably practicable after the body is established; and
  (b) in the case of each subsequent financial year, before the start of the financial year.

(3) The consumer financial education body may, with the approval of the Authority, vary the plan in respect of a financial year at any time after its preparation.

(4) An annual plan in respect of a financial year must set out —
  (a) the objectives of the consumer financial education body for the year;
  (b) how the extent to which each of those objectives is met is to be determined;
  (c) the relative priorities of each of those objectives; and
  (d) how its resources are to be allocated among the activities to be carried on in connection with the discharge of the consumer financial education function.

(5) In sub-paragraph (4) references to objectives for a financial year include objectives for a longer period that includes that year.

(6) Before preparing or varying an annual plan, the consumer financial education body must consult —
  (a) the Treasury;
  (b) the Secretary of State;
  (c) the Office of Fair Trading;
  (d) the Practitioner Panel;
  (e) the Consumer Panel; and

(f) such other persons (if any) as the body considers appropriate.

(7) The consumer financial education body must publish each annual plan, and each variation of an annual plan, in the way it considers appropriate.

Annual reports

9 (1) At least once a year, the consumer financial education body must make a report to the Authority in relation to the discharge of the consumer financial education function.

(2) The report must—
   (a) set out the extent to which the body has met its objectives and priorities for the period covered by the report;
   (b) include a copy of its latest accounts; and
   (c) comply with any requirements specified in rules made by the Authority.

(3) The consumer financial education body must publish each report in the way it considers appropriate.

(4) Nothing in this paragraph requires the consumer financial education body to make a report at any time in the period of 12 months beginning with its establishment.

Exemption from consumer credit rules

10 (1) A licence is not required under Part 3 of the Consumer Credit Act 1974 in respect of anything done by—
   (a) the consumer financial education body in discharging the consumer financial education function; or
   (b) a person acting on its behalf in accordance with arrangements made under paragraph 4(1)(b).

(2) Nothing in Part 4 or 10 of that Act (seeking business or ancillary credit business) is to apply in relation to anything done by—
   (a) the consumer financial education body in discharging the consumer financial education function; or
   (b) a person acting on its behalf in accordance with arrangements made under paragraph 4(1)(b).

PART 2

FUNDING

Meaning of "the relevant costs"

11 (1) In this Part of this Schedule "the relevant costs" means—
   (a) the expenses incurred by the Authority in establishing the consumer financial education body; and
   (b) the expenses incurred, or expected to be incurred, by the consumer financial education body in connection with the discharge of the consumer financial education function.

(2) For the purposes of sub-paragraph (1)(a) it does not matter when the expenses were incurred.

Funding of the relevant costs by authorised persons or payment service providers

12 (1) For the purpose of meeting a proportion of the relevant costs the Authority may makes rules requiring —
    (a) authorised persons or payment service providers, or
    (b) any specified class of authorised person or payment service provider,
    to pay to the Authority specified amounts or amounts calculated in a specified way.

(2) Before making the rules the Authority must have regard to other anticipated sources of funding of the relevant costs.

(3) The amounts to be paid under the rules may include a component to cover the expenses of the Authority in collecting the payments ("collection costs").

(4) The Authority must pay to the consumer financial education body the amounts that it receives under the rules apart from amounts in respect of its collection costs (which it may keep).

(5) "Payment service provider" means a person who is a payment service provider for the purposes of the Payment Services Regulations 2009 as a result of falling within any of paragraphs (a) to (f) of the definition in regulation 2(1).

(6) "Specified" means specified in the rules.

Funding of the relevant costs by consumer credit licensees etc

13 (1) For the purpose of meeting a proportion of the relevant costs the OFT may, with the approval of the Secretary of State and the Treasury, from time to time require —
    (a) qualifying consumer credit licensees or applicants, or
    (b) any specified class of qualifying consumer credit licensee or applicant,
    to pay to the OFT specified amounts or amounts calculated in a specified way.

(2) The requirements are to be imposed by general notice.

(3) "Qualifying consumer credit licensee or applicant" means —
    (a) a licensee under a licence which covers to any extent the carrying on of a type of business specified in an order under section 226A(2)(e); or
    (b) an applicant for a licence, or for the renewal of a licence, which (if granted or renewed) will fall within paragraph (a) above.

(4) Before giving a general notice the OFT must have regard to other anticipated sources of funding of the relevant costs.

(5) Before giving a general notice, the OFT must consult —
    (a) the Authority;

(b) the consumer financial education body; and
(c) such other persons (if any) as the OFT considers appropriate.

(6) The amounts to be paid under a general notice may include a component to cover the expenses of the OFT in collecting the payments ("collection costs").

(7) The OFT must pay to the consumer financial education body the amounts that it receives under a general notice apart from amounts in respect of its collection costs (which it may keep).

(8) A general notice may –
   (a) specify the time at or by which the payments are to be made;
   (b) provide for exceptions from requirements imposed on a class of qualifying consumer credit licensee or applicant;
   (c) impose different requirements on different classes of qualifying consumer credit licensee or applicant;
   (d) make provision for refunds in specified circumstances.

(9) Expressions which are used in sub-paragraph (3) and in the Consumer Credit Act 1974 have the same meaning in that sub-paragraph as in that Act.

(10) In this paragraph –
   "general notice" means a notice published by the OFT at a time and in a manner appearing to it suitable for securing that the notice is seen within a reasonable time by persons likely to be affected by it;
   "the OFT" means the Office of Fair Trading;
   "specified" means specified in the general notice.

Funding by grants or loans etc made by Treasury or Secretary of State

14 (1) The Treasury or the Secretary of State may –
   (a) make grants or loans, or
   (b) provide any other form of financial assistance,
   to the consumer financial education body for the purpose of meeting any expenses incurred by it in connection with the discharge of the consumer financial education function.

(2) Any grant or loan or other form of financial assistance under this paragraph may be made or provided subject to such terms as the Treasury or the Secretary of State consider appropriate.

(3) Any expenses incurred by the Treasury or the Secretary of State under this paragraph are to be met out of money provided by Parliament.

Part 3

Reviews

Reviews of economy etc of the consumer financial education body

15 (1) The Authority may appoint an independent person to conduct a review of the economy, efficiency and effectiveness with which the consumer financial education body has used its resources in discharging the consumer financial education function.

   (2) The Authority must consult the Treasury before acting under this paragraph.

   (3) A review is not to be concerned with the merits of the body's general policy or principles in discharging the consumer financial education function.

   (4) On completion of a review, the person conducting it must make a written report to the Authority —
      (a) setting out the result of the review; and
      (b) making such recommendations (if any) as the person considers appropriate.

   (5) The Authority must publish a copy of the report in the way it considers appropriate.

   (6) Any expenses reasonably incurred in the conduct of the review are to be met by the Authority.

   (7) "Independent" means appearing to the Authority to be independent of the consumer financial education body.

Right to obtain documents and information

16 (1) A person conducting a review under paragraph 15 —
      (a) has a right of access at any reasonable time to all such documents as the person may reasonably require for the purposes of the review; and
      (b) may require any person holding or accountable for any such document to provide such information and explanation as are reasonably required for those purposes.

   (2) This paragraph applies only to documents in the custody or under the control of the consumer financial education body.

   (3) An obligation imposed on a person as a result of this paragraph is enforceable by an injunction or, in Scotland, by an order for specific performance under section 45 of the Court of Session Act 1988."

2 (1) This paragraph applies to rules under paragraph 12 of Schedule 1A to FSMA 2000 (as inserted by this Schedule).

   (2) The FSA may before commencement —
      (a) propose to make rules under that paragraph, and

(b) publish a draft of the proposed rules in the way appearing to it to be best calculated to bring them to the attention of the public.

(3) The draft must be accompanied by —
   (a) an explanation of the purpose of the proposed rules,
   (b) an explanation of the FSA's reasons for believing that making the proposed rules is compatible with its general duties under section 2 of FSMA 2000,
   (c) notice that representations about the proposals may be made to the FSA within a specified time, and
   (d) details of the expected expenditure by reference to which the proposal is made.

(4) Before making the proposed rules after commencement, the FSA must have regard to any representations made to it in accordance with sub-paragraph (3)(c).

(5) If the FSA makes the proposed rules, it must publish an account, in general terms, of —
   (a) the representations made to it in accordance with sub-paragraph (3)(c), and
   (b) its response to them.

(6) If the rules differ from the draft published under sub-paragraph (2) in a way which is, in the FSA's opinion, significant, the FSA must (in addition to complying with sub-paragraph (5)) publish details of the difference.

(7) If the FSA acts in accordance with this paragraph, section 155 of FSMA 2000 (which contains corresponding provision) does not apply.

(8) The FSA may charge a reasonable fee for providing a person with a copy of a draft published under sub-paragraph (2).

(9) In this paragraph —
   "commencement" means the commencement of paragraph 12 of Schedule 1A to FSMA 2000;
   "the FSA" means the Financial Services Authority;
   "FSMA 2000" means the Financial Services and Markets Act 2000.

SCHEDULE 2

Section 24

MINOR AND CONSEQUENTIAL AMENDMENTS

PART 1

AMENDMENTS OF FINANCIAL SERVICES AND MARKETS ACT 2000

1   The Financial Services and Markets Act 2000 is amended as follows.

2   (1) Section 3 (market confidence) is amended as follows.

   (2) In subsection (1), for "the financial system" substitute "the UK financial system".

(3) In subsection (2), for ""The financial system"" substitute "In this Act "the UK financial system"".

3 Until the commencement of the repeal of section 4 (public awareness) by section 2(3) of this Act, section 4 has effect as if—

    (a) the reference in subsection (1) to the financial system were to the UK financial system, and

    (b) subsection (3) were omitted.

4 In section 5 (the protection of consumers), for subsection (3) substitute—

    "(3) Sections 425A and 425B (meaning of "consumers") apply for the purposes of this section."

5 In section 10 (the Consumer Panel), for subsection (7) substitute—

    "(7) Sections 425A and 425B (meaning of "consumers") apply for the purposes of this section, but the references to consumers in this section do not include consumers who are authorised persons."

6 (1) Section 14 (cases in which the Treasury may arrange independent inquiries) is amended as follows.

  (2) In subsection (2)(a), for "the financial system" substitute "the UK financial system".

  (3) For subsection (5) substitute—

    "(5) Sections 425A and 425B (meaning of "consumers") apply for the purposes of this section."

  (4) Omit subsection (6).

7 In the italic cross-heading before section 64, at the end insert "*of approved persons*".

8 (1) Section 66 (performance of regulated activities: disciplinary powers) is amended as follows.

  (2) After subsection (5) insert—

    "(5A) "Approval" means an approval given under section 59."

  (3) In subsection (7), omit "under section 59".

  (4) After that subsection insert—

    "(8) In relation to any time while a suspension is in force under subsection (3)(aa) in relation to part of a function, any reference in section 59 or 63A to the performance of a function includes the performance of part of a function.

    (9) If at any time a restriction imposed under subsection (3)(ab) is contravened, the approval in relation to the person concerned is to be treated for the purposes of sections 59 and 63A as if it had been withdrawn at that time."

9 (1) Section 67 (disciplinary measures: procedure and right to refer to Tribunal) is amended as follows.

(2) In subsection (1), at the end insert "; and if it proposes to take action under subsection (3)(aa) or (ab) of that section, it must also give each of the other interested parties a warning notice."

(3) After subsection (2) insert —

"(2A) A warning notice about a proposal —
   (a) to suspend an approval, or
   (b) to impose a restriction in relation to the performance of a function,
   must state the period for which the suspension or restriction is to have effect."

(4) In subsection (4), at the end insert "; and if it decides to take action under subsection (3)(aa) or (ab) of that section, it must also give each of the other interested parties a decision notice."

(5) After subsection (5) insert —

"(5A) A decision notice about —
   (a) the suspension of an approval, or
   (b) the imposition of a restriction in relation to the performance of a function,
   must state the period for which the suspension or restriction is to have effect."

(6) In subsection (7), at the end insert "; and if the Authority decides to take action under section 66(3)(aa) or (ab), each of the other interested parties may also refer the matter to the Tribunal."

(7) After that subsection insert—

"(8) "Approval" means an approval given under section 59.

(9) "Other interested parties", in relation to an approved person ("A"), are—
   (a) the person on whose application the approval was given ("B"); and
   (b) the person by whom A's services are retained, if not B.
   The reference in this subsection to an approved person has the same meaning as in section 64."

10 (1) Section 69 (statement of policy) is amended as follows.

(2) In subsection (1), for paragraphs (a) and (b) substitute —
   "(a) the imposition of penalties, suspensions or restrictions under section 66;
   (b) the amount of penalties under that section; and
   (c) the period for which suspensions or restrictions under that section are to have effect."

(3) In subsection (2)—
   (a) in the opening words, after "should be" insert ", or what the period for which a suspension or restriction is to have effect should be,", and
   (b) in paragraph (c), for "the person on whom the penalty is to be imposed" substitute "the person against whom action is to be taken".

11 In section 138 (general rule-making power), omit subsections (3) and (7) to (9).

12 In section 150(4) (actions for damages), after paragraph (a) (but before the "or" at the end of it) insert —
    "(aa) rules under section 131B (short selling rules);".

13 In section 155(9) (consultation: exception to general rule that cost benefit analysis required), after paragraph (d) insert —
    "(e) paragraph 12 of Schedule 1A."

14 In section 157 (guidance), after subsection (3) insert —
    "(3A) Subsection (3) also applies in relation to guidance which the Authority proposes to give to persons generally, or to a class of person, in relation to rules under section 131B (short selling rules) to which those persons are subject."

15 In section 165 (FSA's power to require information), in the heading, at the end insert ": authorised persons etc".

16 (1) Section 168 (appointment of persons to carry out investigations in particular cases) is amended as follows.

    (2) In subsection (4), in paragraph (c), for "an authorised person" substitute "a person".

    (3) In that subsection, after paragraph (h) insert —
        "(ha) a person may have performed a controlled function without approval for the purposes of section 63A;".

17 In section 176(11)(a) (entry of premises under warrant), after "165" insert ", 165A, 169A".

18 (1) Section 207 (proposal to take disciplinary measures) is amended as follows.

    (2) In subsection (1), omit the "or" before paragraph (b) and at the end of that paragraph insert "or
        (c) to suspend a permission of an authorised person or impose a restriction in relation to the carrying on of a regulated activity by an authorised person (under section 206A),".

    (3) At the end insert —
        "(4) A warning notice about a proposal to suspend a permission or impose a restriction must state the period for which the suspension or restriction is to have effect."

19 (1) Section 208 (decision notice) is amended as follows.

    (2) In subsection (1), omit the "or" before paragraph (b) and at the end of that paragraph insert "or
        (c) to suspend a permission or impose a restriction under section 206A (whether or not in the manner proposed),".

    (3) After subsection (3) insert —
        "(3A) In the case of a suspension or restriction, the decision notice must state the period for which the suspension or restriction is to have effect."

(4) In subsection (4), omit the "or" before paragraph (b) and at the end of that paragraph insert "or

(c) suspend a permission of an authorised person, or impose a restriction in relation to the carrying on of a regulated activity by an authorised person, under section 206A,".

20 (1) Section 210 (statements of policy) is amended as follows.

(2) In subsection (1), for paragraphs (a) and (b) substitute —

"(a) the imposition of penalties, suspensions or restrictions under this Part;

(b) the amount of penalties under this Part; and

(c) the period for which suspensions or restrictions under this Part are to have effect."

(3) In subsection (2) —

(a) in the opening words, after "should be" insert ", or what the period for which a suspension or restriction is to have effect should be,", and

(b) in paragraph (c), for "the person on whom the penalty is to be imposed" substitute "the person against whom action is to be taken".

(4) In subsection (7), after "206" insert "or 206A".

21 In section 212(2) (the scheme manager), after "those functions" insert "and the functions conferred on it by or under Part 15A".

22 In section 219(3A) (scheme manager's power to require information), for "applying regulations under section 214B(3) above" substitute "determining the matters mentioned in section 214D(2)(a) and (b) above".

23 In section 221A(3) (delegation of functions of FSCS manager), after "management expenses of the scheme manager" insert "except where the function in question is one under Part 15A".

24 (1) Section 223 (FSCS manager's management expenses) is amended as follows.

(2) In subsection (3), in paragraph (c), after "214B" insert "or 214D".

(3) After that paragraph insert —
"(d) under Part 15A."

25 (1) Section 224A (functions under the Banking Act 2009) is amended as follows.

(2) The existing provision becomes subsection (1) of that section.

(3) After that subsection insert —

"(2) Any payment required to be made by the scheme manager by virtue of section 61 of that Act (special resolution regime: compensation) is to be treated for the purposes of this Part as an expense under the compensation scheme."

26 In section 348(5)(d) (restrictions on disclosure of confidential information by Authority etc), after "a person appointed" insert "to collect or update information under section 139E or".

27 In section 354 (FSA's duty to co-operate with others), after subsection (1A)

insert—

"(1B) In pursuing its financial stability objective, the Authority must take such steps as it considers appropriate to co-operate with other relevant bodies (including the Treasury and the Bank of England)."

28   In section 391 (publication), for subsection (11) substitute—

"(11) Section 425A (meaning of "consumers") applies for the purposes of this section."

29 (1) Section 392 (warning and decision notices: third party rights and access to evidence) is amended as follows.

(2) In paragraph (a)—
   (a) after "63(3)," insert "63B(1),", and
   (b) after "126(1)," insert "131H(1),".

(3) In paragraph (b)—
   (a) after "63(4)," insert "63B(3),", and
   (b) after "127(1)," insert "131H(4),".

30   After section 415 insert—

"Powers of the Authority

415A Powers of the Authority

Any power which the Authority has under any provision of this Act is not limited in any way by any other power which it has under any other provision of this Act."

31   In section 417(1) (definitions), after the definition of "UK authorised person" (but before the "and" at the end of it) insert—

""the UK financial system" has the meaning given in section 3;".

32   After section 425 insert—

"425A Consumers: regulated activities etc carried on by authorised persons

(1) This section has effect for the purposes of the provisions of this Act which apply this section.

(2) "Consumers" means persons who—
   (a) use, have used or may use any of the services within subsection (3); or
   (b) have relevant rights or interests in relation to any of those services.

(3) The services within this subsection are services provided by—
   (a) authorised persons in carrying on regulated activities;
   (b) authorised persons who are investment firms, or credit institutions, in providing relevant ancillary services; or
   (c) persons acting as appointed representatives.

(4) A person ("P") has a "relevant right or interest" in relation to any services within subsection (3) if P has a right or interest—

(a) which is derived from, or is otherwise attributable to, the use of the services by others; or

(b) which may be adversely affected by the use of the services by persons acting on P's behalf or in a fiduciary capacity in relation to P.

(5) If a person is providing a service within subsection (3) as a trustee, the persons who are, have been or may be beneficiaries of the trust are to be treated as persons who use, have used or may use the service.

(6) A person who deals with another person ("A") in the course of A providing a service within subsection (3) is to be treated as using the service.

(7) In this section —

"credit institution" means —

(a) a credit institution authorised under the banking consolidation directive; or

(b) an institution which would satisfy the requirements for authorisation as a credit institution under that directive if it had its registered office (or if does not have one, its head office) in an EEA State;

"relevant ancillary service" means any service of a kind mentioned in Section B of Annex I to the markets in financial instruments directive the provision of which does not involve the carrying on of a regulated activity.

425B Consumers: regulated activities carried on by others

(1) This section has effect for the purposes of the provisions of this Act which apply this section.

(2) "Consumers" means persons who, in relation to regulated activities carried on otherwise than by authorised persons, would be consumers as defined by section 425A if the activities were carried on by authorised persons."

33 (1) Section 429 (Parliamentary control of statutory instruments) is amended as follows.

(2) In subsection (1)(a) —

(a) omit "404", and

(b) after "236(5)," insert "404G".

(3) In subsection (2), after "214B" insert ", 214D".

(4) In subsection (8), after "one made under section" insert "165A(2)(d) or".

34 (1) Schedule 1 (general provision about the FSA) is amended as follows.

(2) In paragraph 5(2)(a), after "paragraph 1(2)(a) to (d)" insert "or in determining or reviewing its strategy in relation to the financial stability objective".

(3) After paragraph 19A insert—

"Amounts required by rules to be paid to the Authority

19B   Any amount (other than a fee) which is required by rules to be paid to the Authority may be recovered as a debt due to the Authority."

35 (1) In Schedule 4 (treaty rights), paragraph 1 is amended as follows.

(2) The existing provision becomes sub-paragraph (1) of that paragraph.

(3) In that sub-paragraph, omit the definition of "consumers".

(4) After that sub-paragraph insert—

"(2) Section 425A (meaning of "consumers") applies for the purposes of this Schedule."

PART 2

AMENDMENTS OF OTHER LEGISLATION

Consumer Credit Act 1974

36   In section 25(2A)(b) of the Consumer Credit Act 1974 (evidence as to whether a licensee is a fit person), after sub-paragraph (i) insert—

"(ia)   paragraph 13 of Schedule 1A to the Financial Services and Markets Act 2000;".

Contracting Out (Functions Relating to National Savings) Order 1998

37   In article 3 of the Contracting Out (Functions Relating to National Savings) Order 1998 (contracting out of functions), after paragraph (2) insert—

"(3) Any function conferred on the Director under rules made under section 38(7) of the Administration of Justice Act 1982 (court funds rules) may be exercised by, or by employees of, such person (if any) as may be authorised in that behalf by the Director."

Financial Services and Markets Act 2000 (Markets in Financial Instruments) (Modification of Powers) Regulations 2006

38   In the Financial Services and Markets Act 2000 (Markets in Financial Instruments) (Modification of Powers) Regulations 2006, omit regulation 3(b)(ii) (which made an amendment of the Financial Services and Markets Act 2000 superseded by this Act).

Banking Act 2009

39   The Banking Act 2009 is amended as follows.

40   In section 1(6) (table describing provisions of Part 1), in the entry relating to sections 33 to 48, for "48" substitute "48A".

41   In section 61(2)(b) (sources of compensation), for the words from "subject" to "below)," substitute "subject to section 214C of the Financial Services and Markets Act 2000 (limit on amount of special resolution regime payments),".

42 In section 83(2)(h) (supplemental), omit "- inserted by section 171 below".

43 Omit section 171 (which made amendments of the Financial Services and Markets Act 2000 superseded by this Act).

44 In section 183(c) (interpretation of expressions for purposes of Part 5), omit "to "the financial system"".

45 In section 204(1)(a) (inter-bank payment systems: information), after "order" insert "or an order under section 206A".

46 Omit section 248 (which made an amendment of the Financial Services and Markets Act 2000 superseded by this Act).

47 In section 250(2) (collection of information by FSA relevant to financial stability) —
   (a) after "section 165" insert "or 165A", and
   (b) after "as qualified" insert ", in the case of the section 165 power,".

48 (1) Section 259 (statutory instruments) is amended as follows.

   (2) In the table in subsection (3), omit the entry relating to section 171.

   (3) In that table, after the entry relating to section 204 insert —

"206A	Services forming part of recognised inter-bank payment systems	Draft affirmative resolution"

   (4) In subsection (5), omit paragraph (o) and the "and" before it.

© Crown copyright 2010

These notes refer to the Financial Services Act 2010 (c.28) which received Royal Assent on 8 April 2010

FINANCIAL SERVICES ACT 2010

EXPLANATORY NOTES

INTRODUCTION

1. These Explanatory Notes relate to the Financial Services Act which received Royal Assent on 8 April. They have been prepared by the Treasury in order to assist the reader in understanding the Act. They do not form part of the Act and have not been endorsed by Parliament.

2. These Notes need to be read in conjunction with the Act. They are not, and are not meant to be, a comprehensive description of the Act. So where a section or part of a section does not seem to require any explanation or comment, none is given.

BACKGROUND TO THE ACT

3. In 1997, the Government proposed a new system of financial regulation in the UK. A structure for overseeing the UK financial system was created, with distinct roles for HM Treasury, the Bank of England and the Financial Services Authority ("the FSA") (together, "the relevant authorities") and distinct responsibilities for overall financial stability issues, which are set out in a memorandum of understanding between the relevant authorities.

4. The Bank of England Act 1998 established the arrangements for the Bank's current monetary policy responsibilities. Under the 1998 Act, the banking supervision function that had previously been undertaken by the Bank was transferred to the FSA.

5. The Financial Services and Markets Act 2000 ("FSMA") set out the framework within which the FSA operates, as the single regulator for the financial services industry. It also established the framework for the Financial Services Compensation Scheme ("the FSCS") to provide compensation for consumers in the event that a financial services firm is unable to meet its obligations to them.

6. The Banking Act 2009 built on this framework to enhance the ability of the relevant authorities to deal with crises in the banking system, to protect depositors and to maintain financial stability. The Act established a new permanent special resolution regime, providing the relevant authorities with a range of tools to deal with banks and building societies that are failing.

These notes refer to the Financial Services Act 2010 (c.28) which received Royal Assent on 8 April 2010

7. In July 2009 the Treasury published *Reforming financial markets*[1], which proposed reforms to financial regulation to enable more effective prudential regulation and supervision of firms, greater emphasis on monitoring and managing system-wide risks, and improved protection and support for consumers. In this document and following a review of consultation responses, the Government announced its intention to bring forward legislation on the following.

SUMMARY AND OVERVIEW OF THE STRUCTURE OF THE ACT

Objectives of FSA etc

8. FSMA currently sets out four objectives for the FSA. These are: maintaining confidence in the financial system; promoting public understanding of the financial system; securing the appropriate degree of protection for consumers; and reducing financial crime. As maintaining financial stability is a fundamental component of maintaining confidence in the financial system, the Act provides the FSA with an additional objective, namely an explicit financial stability objective. In considering financial stability, the FSA must have regard to the costs to the economy both of instability and of regulatory actions (taken to reduce instability). The FSA, like the Bank of England, is required to consult the Treasury when determining its strategy for financial stability.

9. The Act removes the FSA's regulatory objective of promoting public understanding of the financial system and requires the FSA to establish a new consumer financial education body whose purpose is to raise the understanding and knowledge of members of the public of financial matters (including the financial system) and improve their ability to manage their financial affairs. The new body will therefore take over responsibility for the activity previously undertaken by the FSA as part of the National Strategy for Financial Capability under its 'public understanding' objective. In addition the body will implement the national rollout of an impartial generic financial advice or 'money guidance' service, taking forward the recommendations of the Thoresen Review[2].

10. The Act provides that the FSA's powers, including its general rule-making power, can now be exercised for the purpose of meeting any of its regulatory objectives. Previously, these powers were only exercisable in pursuit of its consumer protection objective.

---

[1] *Reforming financial markets*, HM Treasury, 8 July 2009. http://www.hm-treasury.gov.uk/d/reforming_financial_markets080709.pdf
[2] *Thoresen Review of Generic Financial Advice: Final Report*, HM Treasury, 3 March 2009. http://www.hm-treasury.gov.uk/d/thoresenreview_final.pdf

*These notes refer to the Financial Services Act 2010 (c.28)
which received Royal Assent on 8 April 2010*

Remuneration of executives of authorised persons

11. The Act gives the Treasury power to make provision for executive remuneration reports, and imposes a new duty on the FSA to make general rules requiring authorised persons (or a specified class of authorised persons) to have and implement a remuneration policy and to secure that the remuneration policy satisfies the requirements set out in the Act. It also provides the FSA with other powers in relation to remuneration.

Recovery and resolution plans

12. The Act imposes on the FSA a duty to make rules requiring the production of recovery and resolution plans by authorised persons (or certain classes of authorised person) and makes other provision about such plans. A recovery plan aims to reduce the likelihood of failure of a firm by setting out what the authorised person would do in, or prior to it becoming subject to, stressed circumstances (which the FSA may specify in its rules) that would affect the ability of the authorised person to carry on all or a significant part of its business. A resolution plan is a plan covering both action to be taken in the event of failure of all or any part of the business occurring and action to be taken by a firm where failure is likely. This would include action to be taken by the relevant authorities to resolve the authorised person.

Short selling

13. The Act provides the FSA with a new power to prohibit, or require disclosure of, short selling.

FSA's disciplinary powers

14. The Act provides the FSA with greater enforcement powers. The FSA has the power to fine authorised persons and approved individuals for misconduct. The Act extends these powers to enable the FSA to suspend or limit an authorised person's permission or an approved person's approval. It also enables the FSA to impose a fine on an individual performing a controlled function without approval, as well as prohibit the individual from working in the industry. Additionally, it includes provisions concerning disclosure by the FSA of decision notices.

Measures to protect consumers

15. The Act enables the FSA to make rules requiring firms to establish consumer redress schemes. Rules can be made if it appears to the FSA that (a) there may have been a widespread or regular failure by a relevant firm to comply with the requirements for carrying on an activity; (b) as a result, consumers have suffered or may suffer loss that would entitle them to redress; and (c) it is desirable to establish a scheme to secure redress for consumers.

16. The Act makes it an offence for a credit card issuer to provide credit card cheques to a customer, other than in response to a request from that customer.

*These notes refer to the Financial Services Act 2010 (c.28)
which received Royal Assent on 8 April 2010*

Financial Services Compensation Scheme (FSCS)

17. The FSCS is the scheme established by the FSA under Part 15 of FSMA to compensate customers of authorised financial services firms when those firms are in default, that is, unable or likely to be unable to pay claims.

18. Under section 214B of FSMA, which was inserted by the Banking Act 2009, the Treasury may require the FSCS to contribute to the costs incurred in applying the stabilisation powers of the special resolution regime (established in Part 1 of the Banking Act) to a bank that is failing. The Act replaces section 214B and inserts two new sections into FSMA to provide that the "expenses" to which the FSCS may be required to contribute include interest, and that the limit up to which the FSCS may be required to contribute (which reflects the amount the FSCS would have had to pay out had no stabilisation power been used and the bank been unable to satisfy claims against it) takes into account the costs that the FSCS would have incurred in funding compensation payments if the stabilisation power had not been exercised.

19. The Act inserts a new Part 15A into FSMA to enable the Treasury to require the FSCS manager to make payments on behalf of another compensation scheme (or a government or other authority) that pays compensation in respect of institutions that provide financial services, including institutions that are not authorised financial services firms under FSMA.

Powers to require information

20. The Act confers on the FSA a power to require certain types of person to provide specified information, where the FSA considers that the information or documents in question are or might be relevant to the stability of one or more aspects of the financial system.

21. The Act provides the Treasury with the power to require information or documents from participants or proposed participants in the Asset Protection Scheme or related schemes.

Banking Act 2009

22. The Act makes some minor and technical amendments to the Banking Act 2009, including amendments that (a) make express that the property transfer power can be used to impose a liability on a residual company in place of liabilities transferred from the residual company; and (b) allow compensation orders (see section 49 for the various orders that may be made) to include an independent valuer order in the interests of administrative efficiency.

Director of Savings

23. The Act provides for the Director of Savings to undertake functions on behalf of the Accountant General for England and Wales where appointed to do so under court funds rules.

*These notes refer to the Financial Services Act 2010 (c.28)
which received Royal Assent on 8 April 2010*

TERRITORIAL EXTENT

24. The Act extends to the whole of the UK.

25. At Introduction the Bill for this Act contained provisions that triggered the Sewel Convention. The provisions relate to the establishment of a consumer education body. The Sewel Convention provides that Westminster will not normally legislate with regard to devolved matters in Scotland without the consent of the Scottish Parliament. Legislative consent was obtained from the Scottish Parliament.

ANNEX

26. The Annex lists the standard abbreviations of enactments and technical terms used in these notes.

COMMENTARY ON SECTIONS AND SCHEDULES

Objectives of FSA etc

Section 1: Financial stability objective

27. This section amends section 2 of FSMA to give the FSA an additional regulatory objective (or 'general duty') concerning financial stability. It inserts a new section 3A in FSMA, which provides that the objective is to contribute to the protection and enhancement of the stability of the UK financial system. This is similar to the financial stability objective of the Bank of England under section 2A of the Bank of England Act 1998 (inserted by section 238 of the Banking Act 2009).

28. New section 3A of FSMA requires the FSA, in considering this objective, to have regard to the economic and fiscal consequences of instability and also to any effects on economic growth of regulatory actions taken for stability reasons. In addition the FSA, in considering this objective, must have regard to the possible impact on UK financial stability of events and circumstances outside the UK. The section also requires the FSA to develop and keep under review a strategy concerning this objective, in consultation with the Treasury.

29. *Schedule 2* makes consequential amendments to FSMA. Paragraph 2 of that Schedule substitutes the term "the UK financial system" for "the financial system" in section 3(1) of FSMA (which deals with the "market confidence" objective) and provides a definition of that term in section 3(2) of FSMA. Similar substitutions are made by paragraphs 3 and 6(2) to sections 4 and 14 of FSMA respectively. Paragraph 31 amends section 417 of FSMA (definitions) to clarify that the definition of "UK financial system" in section 3(2) of FSMA applies for the purposes of that Act.

*These notes refer to the Financial Services Act 2010 (c.28)
which received Royal Assent on 8 April 2010*

Section 2: Enhancing public understanding of financial matters etc

30. *Subsections (2)(a) and (3)* of this section remove the FSA's regulatory objective of promoting public understanding of the financial system. *Subsection (2)(b)* requires the FSA to have regard to the desirability of enhancing the understanding and knowledge of the public of financial matters when the FSA discharges its general functions set out in section 2(4) of FSMA.

31. *Subsection (4)* requires the FSA, when discharging its consumer protection regulatory objective, to have regard to information provided to the FSA by the new consumer financial education body to be established under new section 6A of FSMA.

32. *Subsection (5)* inserts a new section 6A in FSMA which imposes an obligation on the FSA to establish a body, referred to as the consumer financial education body (the "CFEB"). The CFEB's function is defined in new section 6A and the main purposes are to help members of the public to:

    - better understand financial matters; and

    - improve their ability to manage their own financial affairs.

33. New section 6A(2) provides illustrations of the types of activity the CFEB might carry out in accordance with its function under new section 6A(1). This includes delivering the money guidance service and programmes to improve financial capability in the UK. New section 6A(2)(e) allows CFEB to deliver information and advice to members of the public. "Advice" has an ordinary meaning and does not include advice which is regulated under FSMA.

34. *Subsection (6)* introduces Schedule 1, which inserts new Schedule 1A into FSMA. Schedule 1A makes further provision for the establishment and operation of the CFEB.

35. *Paragraph 1* requires the FSA to ensure that the CFEB can undertake the activities set out in new section 6A. The FSA has a number of responsibilities under this schedule, including appointing the board, approving the CFEB's annual budget and annual plan, and making rules for the collection from FSA-regulated firms of amounts towards the CFEB's establishment and running costs. *Paragraph 1(2)* enables the FSA to provide services (such as HR or IT support) to the CFEB.

36. *Paragraph 2* provides that the CFEB must have a chair, a chief executive and a board, and that these persons (who are the CFEB's directors) are appointed by the FSA (in the case of the chair and chief executive, with the agreement of the Treasury). The FSA has the power to remove any member from the board (acting, in the case of the chair and chief executive of the board, with the agreement of the Treasury), but the terms of each board member's appointment (e.g. length of appointment, the basis on which they may be dismissed) must be sufficient for the director (and the board) to be independent from the FSA. The FSA can only appoint someone to the CFEB board if

satisfied that the person has knowledge or experience likely to be relevant to the CFEB's function.

37. Paragraph 3 provides that the CFEB and its members and employees will not be acting on behalf of the Crown and its employees will not be civil servants.

38. Paragraph 4 makes it clear that the CFEB can arrange for others to act on the CFEB's behalf as the CFEB's agent in delivering its consumer financial education function or can support others in undertaking activities which would fall within the CFEB's function. This can include providing financial support and payment to others to undertake such activities.

39. Paragraph 5 permits a body to undertake work for the CFEB even where it would otherwise not be able to do so. This would enable bodies (such as those established by royal charter or with limited charitable aims) to operate where otherwise their constitution may not permit them to do so.

40. Paragraph 6 requires the CFEB when exercising its function to have regard to the importance of maintaining confidence in the financial system and the stability of the financial system.

41. Paragraph 7 requires the CFEB to prepare a budget before the beginning of each financial year (or in its first year, as quickly as is reasonably practicable) and for the budget to be approved by the FSA. When preparing the budget or planning to vary it the CFEB must consult the persons listed in *sub-paragraph (4)*. The CFEB may vary a budget which has been adopted, with the agreement of the FSA. It is anticipated that, in addition to the sums received by exercising the powers given to the FSA under paragraph 12 and the OFT under paragraph 13, the CFEB may receive public funds under paragraph 14. It is also anticipated that sums will be provided to the CFEB pursuant to directions issued under section 22 of the Dormant Bank and Building Society Accounts Act 2008. As the provisions of paragraphs 12 and 13 make clear, the FSA and the OFT respectively are required to take into account other anticipated sources of funding when fixing a levy on FSA-regulated and OFT-licensed firms. The CFEB is also required to publish each budget or variation of the budget, in a way the CFEB considers appropriate.

42. Paragraph 8 requires the CFEB to prepare an annual plan before the beginning of each financial year (or in its first year, as quickly as is reasonably possible) setting out its objectives (both long and short term), the priority to be given to each objective, how it intends to allocate its resources and the tools it will use in determining the extent to which its objectives have been met. It may vary its plan at any point during that year. The annual plan and any variation of it must be approved by the FSA. When preparing the annual plan or planning to vary it the CFEB must consult the persons listed in *sub-paragraph (6)*. The CFEB is also required to publish each annual plan or variation of the annual plan, in a way the CFEB considers appropriate.

43. *Paragraph 9* requires the CFEB to prepare a report, at least annually, on its activities, setting out how it has met the objectives and priorities set out in the annual plan for the period covered by the report and annexing its latest accounts. The CFEB has to publish each report in the way it considers appropriate.

44. *Paragraph 10* exempts the CFEB and those acting on its behalf from the requirement to obtain a licence under Part 3 of the Consumer Credit Act 1974 ("CCA"). A licence is required under Part 3 for businesses (with certain exceptions) to carry on consumer credit, consumer hire or ancillary credit business. *Sub-paragraph (2)* disapplies Parts 4 and 10 of the CCA to the CFEB and those acting on its behalf. Part 4 of the CCA relates to advertising and other aspects of seeking credit business and Part 10 relates to ancillary credit business. These provisions are included because the CFEB may on occasion engage in activities which could fall within the ambit of these Parts of the CCA, for example, if a CFEB staff member or one of CFEB's agents were to help an individual to use an online credit card comparison tool during a Money Guidance session, this could be 'credit brokerage' and fall within the definition of ancillary credit business in Part 10.

45. *Paragraph 11* defines "relevant costs" for the purpose of Part 2 of Schedule 1A to mean the expenses the FSA incurs in establishing the CFEB and the costs incurred or to be incurred by the CFEB.

46. *Paragraph 12* gives the FSA the power to levy sums from persons authorised under FSMA and certain payment service providers defined in the Payment Services Regulations 2009 to meet part of the "relevant costs". The FSA levies by way of making rules to required authorised persons or payment services providers specified in the rules to pay sums to the FSA to meet the "relevant costs". The FSA will determine the amount to be levied but under *sub-paragraph (2)* must take into account other anticipated funding for the CFEB before making its rules. The FSA is required to pay sums it collects to the CFEB, but can deduct from such sums the costs of collecting the money.

47. *Paragraph 13* gives the OFT power to levy CCA licence holders and applicants for such licences to meet part of the "relevant costs". *Sub-paragraph (3)* defines the type of consumer credit licensees and applicants who can be included in a levy, by referring to those persons specified in an order made under section 226A(2)(e) of FSMA (which specifies types of business to be included in the consumer credit jurisdiction of the Financial Ombudsman Scheme). The OFT levies by way of a general notice to the relevant licence holders or applicants. Under *sub-paragraph (4)*, the OFT must take into account other anticipated funding for the CFEB before issuing a general notice. *Sub-paragraph (5)* requires the OFT to consult the FSA, the CFEB and any other relevant persons before issuing a general notice. The OFT is also required to pay sums it collects to the CFEB, but can deduct from such sums the costs of collecting the money. *Sub-paragraph (8)* makes it clear that a general notice can impose different requirements on different licence holders or applicants and can exempt persons from a requirement to pay sums.

These notes refer to the Financial Services Act 2010 (c.28) which received Royal Assent on 8 April 2010

48. Paragraph 14 gives the Treasury and the Secretary of State the power to make grants or loans or provide other financial assistance to the CFEB. It is intended that the powers of the Secretary of State in this Schedule will be exercised by the Secretary of State for Business, Innovation and Skills.

49. Paragraph 15 enables the FSA to appoint an independent reviewer to review the efficiency of the CFEB's use of its resources. The FSA must consult the Treasury before making such an appointment. The reviewer must set out the results of the review and any recommendations in a written report. The FSA must publish the report in the way it considers appropriate and must meet the expenses of the review.

50. Paragraph 16 provides the independent reviewer appointed under paragraph 15 with the right of access to documents and information held by the CFEB which are reasonably required for the review.

51. Subsection (7) provides that if staff of the FSA are transferred to the CFEB the Transfer of Undertakings (Protection of Employment) Regulations 2006 will apply to such a transfer.

Section 3: Meeting FSA's regulatory objectives

52. This section amends four sections of FSMA so as to broaden the ends towards which the FSA can use its rule-making, permission-varying and intervention powers. As a result of this section, these powers will be exercisable for the purpose of meeting any of the FSA's regulatory objectives and not just the consumer protection objective.

53. Subsection (2) amends section 44 of FSMA, which deals with the FSA's power to vary or cancel an authorised person's permission (to undertake a regulated activity) at their request. The amendment to section 44(3) provides that the FSA may refuse an application if this is desirable to meet any of its regulatory objectives.

54. Subsection (3) amends section 45 of FSMA, which concerns the FSA's power, on its own initiative, to modify or cancel an authorised person's permission. *Subsection (3)(a)* substitutes a new *subsection (1)(c)* which enables the FSA to use this power in pursuit of any of its regulatory objectives. *Subsection (3)(b)* inserts a provision making clear that the consumers being protected by the exercise of the power need not be consumers of services of the authorised person whose permission is being varied.

55. Subsection (4) amends section 138 of FSMA to enable the FSA to use its general rule-making power in pursuit of any of its regulatory objectives.

56. Subsection (5) amends section 194 of FSMA, which concerns the FSA's power to intervene in relation to an incoming firm from another EEA state. *Subsection (5)(a)* substitutes a new subsection (1)(c) enabling the FSA to use this power in pursuit of any of its regulatory objectives. *Subsection (5)(b)* makes an amendment to clarify that the power may be exercised to protect consumers who need not be consumers of the services of the firm in respect of which the FSA is intervening.

57. Schedule 2 makes consequential amendments to FSMA. These include paragraph 32 which inserts new sections 425A and 425B into FSMA, which contain definitions of "consumers" and paragraphs 11 and 35(3), which remove the existing definitions of "consumers" from section 138 of, and Schedule 4 to, FSMA respectively. Paragraphs 4, 5, 6(3), 28 and 35(4) of this Schedule insert provisions applying the definitions in new sections 425A and 425B of FSMA (as appropriate) for the purposes of sections 5, 10, 14, 391 of, and Schedule 4 to, FSMA respectively.

Remuneration of executives of authorised persons

Section 4: Executives' remuneration reports

58. This section gives the Treasury the power to make regulations requiring the preparation of a report disclosing information on the remuneration paid to officers and employees of a person who is an authorised person under FSMA and to others with a specified connection to the authorised person. Quoted companies are already required to produce and publish a directors' remuneration report detailing all monies paid to executive and non-executive directors. This section gives the Treasury power to expand the disclosure regime beyond quoted companies, and to employees who are not directors.

59. *Subsection (1)* gives the Treasury power to make regulations on executive remuneration reports.

60. *Subsection (2)* defines "executive remuneration report" for the purposes of this section.

61. *Subsection (3)* lists the type of persons who can be considered to be executives for the purposes of the executives' remuneration report. They include any individual who has a connection with the authorised person which is specified in the regulations made by the Treasury. *Subsection (4)* provides further information on who may fall into this last category and makes it clear that the Treasury is able to require the disclosure of information in relation to remuneration given to individuals providing services to an authorised person who are not employees of that person.

62. *Subsection (5)* means that the Treasury can make regulations imposing disclosure requirements on a class of authorised person defined in the regulations. "Authorised person" is a term which encompasses a wide range of financial institutions and individuals in the financial services industry. Regulations may be made in relation to one or more sections of the financial services industry.

63. *Subsection (6)* provides that regulations made under this section must be made using the affirmative resolution procedure.

Section 5: Executives' remuneration reports: supplementary

64. This section details supplementary provisions in relation to section 4.

65. Subsection *(1)* makes it clear that the Treasury can make provision regarding the information which is required to be included, the manner in which the information is presented, and what information has to be audited.

66. Subsection *(2)* provides that the Treasury may require the executive remuneration report to contain any information corresponding to information which quoted companies could be required to include in directors' remuneration reports by regulations made by the Secretary of State under section 421 of the Companies Act 2006. The requirements for directors' remuneration reports are currently set out in Schedule 8 to the Large and Medium-sized Companies and Groups (Accounts and Reports) Regulations 2008 (S.I. 2008/410). The Treasury may also require the disclosure of comparative information, such as the ratio between the highest and lowest paid employees.

67. Subsection *(3)* provides that the Treasury can require executive remuneration reports to be filed with registrars of companies or the FSA, and provides that the FSA may publish reports filed with it.

68. Subsection *(4)* provides that regulations made by the Treasury may apply any provisions made in or under the Companies Act 2006 in respect of directors' remuneration reports to executive remuneration reports, with appropriate modifications. Under *subsection (5)* this includes provisions creating offences for failure to comply with the requirements for directors' remuneration reports. However, it also makes it clear that the Treasury may not impose stricter penalties for offences applied to executive remuneration reports than the original offence in relation to directors' remuneration reports.

69. Under *subsection (6)* the Treasury may provide that any requirements imposed on authorised persons in the regulations are to be treated as requirements imposed on that person under FSMA. The result of such a provision would be that, if the authorised person contravened a requirement under the regulations, the disciplinary powers of the FSA under FSMA would apply, and the FSA would be able to take action against the authorised person in question.

70. Subsection *(7)* defines terms in sections 4 and 5 for the purposes of these sections.

Section 6: Remuneration rules made by FSA

71. This section inserts a new section 139A into FSMA, which imposes a new duty on the FSA in relation to remuneration.

New section 139A: General rules about remuneration

72. Subsection *(1)* imposes a duty on the FSA to make rules requiring authorised persons under FSMA, or a class of authorised persons identified in FSA rules, to have and implement a remuneration policy.

These notes refer to the Financial Services Act 2010 (c.28) which received Royal Assent on 8 April 2010

73. *Subsection (2)* defines what a "remuneration policy" is for the purposes of this section. It also lists the types of person that may be included within the scope of the authorised person's remuneration policy. They include officers, employees and any other persons of a description specified in the FSA rules.

74. *Subsection (3)* obliges the FSA to ensure, through its rules, that remuneration policies required by the rules are consistent with the effective management of risks and the Financial Stability Boards' Principles for Sound Compensation Practices Implementation Standards.

75. *Subsection (4)* means that in making rules about remuneration the FSA must have regard to any other relevant international standards about remuneration which are in force.

76. *Subsection (5)* gives the Treasury power to direct the FSA to consider whether the remuneration plans of those authorised persons described or listed in the direction comply with the requirements the FSA have imposed in relation to remuneration policies. Under *subsection (6)* the FSA must be consulted before the Treasury make such a direction.

77. *Subsection (7)* provides that where the FSA considers that a remuneration policy fails to meet these requirements, the FSA must take such steps as it considers appropriate to deal with the failure. *Subsection (8)* makes clear that the steps the FSA may take include requiring the revision of the relevant remuneration policy.

78. *Subsection (9)* provides that FSA rules may impose specific prohibitions on the way in which a person may be remunerated. They may provide that any provision of a remuneration contract which contravenes such a prohibition is void and so unenforceable, and make provision for the recovery of any payment which may have been made under such a provision.

79. *Subsection (10)* limits the FSA's power to impose such prohibitions by requiring that it may only be used to ensure consistency with the matters mentioned there.

80. *Subsection (11)* clarifies that a rule made by the FSA under *subsection (9)* which provides that a contractual provision which contravenes a prohibition on remuneration is void will not affect any provision contained in an agreement which was made before the date the rules containing the prohibition were made. Only subsequent amendments to pre-existing contracts, and contracts made after that date, will be affected.

81. *Subsection (12)* defines terms used in this section.

82. *Subsection (13)* means that the references to "the Implementation Standards" or "international standards" in this section are references to standards that are currently in force.

Recovery and resolution plans (RRPs)

Section 7: Rules made by FSA about recovery and resolution plans

83. Section 7(1) inserts new sections 139B to 139F into FSMA. The new provisions place a duty on the FSA to make rules requiring the production of recovery and resolution plans (RRPs); give the FSA additional enforcement powers related to collection of information in relation to RRPs; require the FSA to have regard to international developments in making rules around RRPs; and require the FSA to consult the Bank of England and the Treasury in relation to the drafting of rules for RRPs of banking institutions and (in the case of resolution plans prepared by those institutions) assessment of those plans by the relevant authorities.

New section 139B - Rules about recovery plans

84. *Subsection (1)* places a duty on the FSA to make rules requiring persons authorised under FSMA to produce and maintain a recovery plan in accordance with the requirements set out in the rules. Subject to subsection (8), this requirement can apply to all authorised persons or the FSA can exercise discretion over which authorised persons are required to produce a recovery plan by specifying the firms to which the rules apply. This will allow for gradual implementation, focusing on the largest, most complex and systemically significant firms in the first instance.

85. *Subsections (2), (3)* and *(4)* define a 'recovery plan' for the purposes of the new provisions. A recovery plan aims to reduce the likelihood of failure of a firm by setting out what the authorised person would do in, or prior to it becoming subject to, stressed circumstances (which the FSA may specify in its rules) that would affect the ability of the authorised person to carry on all or a specified part of its business. Action described in the plan may include the restructuring, scaling back or sale of certain business lines or assets of the authorised person in question and the subsection therefore refers to the business not necessarily having to be carried on in the same way or by the same person. The plan is not to be for the purpose of helping an authorised person to plan for avoiding getting into difficult circumstances, but about what planning they can do to enable them to recover should they encounter such circumstances.

86. *Subsection (5)* requires the FSA to consider whether each recovery plan required by rules under subsection (1) makes satisfactory provision in relation to those matters that the plan is required to cover.

87. *Subsection (6)* provides that where the FSA considers that a recovery plan fails to make satisfactory provision in relation to those matters, the FSA must take such steps as it considers appropriate to deal with the failure. *Subsection (7)* makes clear that the steps the FSA may take include requiring the revision of the relevant recovery plan.

These notes refer to the Financial Services Act 2010 (c.28) which received Royal Assent on 8 April 2010

88. *Subsection (8)* requires the FSA to make general rules about recovery plans that apply to authorised persons in relation to whom any power under Part 1 of the Banking Act 2009 may be exercised. The FSA is required by *subsection (9)* to consult the Treasury and Bank of England before preparing a draft of those general rules.

New section 139C – Rules about resolution plans

89. *Subsection (1)* places a duty on the FSA to make rules requiring persons authorised under FSMA to produce and maintain a resolution plan in accordance with the requirements set out in the rules. Subject to subsection (9), this requirement can apply to all authorised persons or the FSA can exercise discretion over which authorised persons are required to produce a recovery plan by specifying the firms to which the rules apply. This will allow for gradual implementation, focusing on the largest, most complex and systemically significant firms in the first instance.

90. *Subsections (2), (3)* and *(4)* define a 'resolution plan'. They clarify that a "resolution plan" should cover both action to be taken in the event of failure of all or any part of the business occurring, and action to be taken by a firm where failure is likely.

91. *Subsection (4)* clarifies that a resolution plan may require a firm to identify obstacles to the application of possible resolution tools by the authorities or to the carrying out of the functions of an insolvency official in the event of the authorised person's failure and to set out what action that may be required to facilitate the application of those tools or carrying out of those functions. This could include provisions to ensure that a 'data room' can be set up quickly and effectively. It could also mean information about the simplification of legal structures ahead of a resolution being triggered.

92. *Subsection (5)* makes clear that information that would facilitate planning by the Treasury or Bank of England in relation to the possible exercise of their powers under Part 1, 2 or 3 of the Banking Act 2009 may be required by rules to be included in a resolution plan.

93. *Subsection (6)* requires the FSA to consider whether each resolution plan makes satisfactory provision in relation to those matters that the plan is required to cover.

94. *Subsection (7)* provides that where the FSA considers that a resolution plan fails to make satisfactory provision in relation to those matters, the FSA must take such steps as it considers appropriate to deal with the failure. *Subsection (8)* makes clear that the steps the FSA may take include requiring the revision of the relevant resolution plan.

95. *Subsection (9* requires the FSA to make general rules about resolution plans that apply to authorised persons in relation to whom any power under Part 1 of the Banking Act 2009 may be exercised. The FSA is required by *subsection (10)* to consult the Treasury and Bank of England before preparing a draft of those general rules.

*These notes refer to the Financial Services Act 2010 (c.28)
which received Royal Assent on 8 April 2010*

New section 139D – Sections 139B and 139C: interpretation

96. *Subsection (1)* clarifies that references in new section 139B and new section 139C (see subsection (3) in each case) to taking action include action not only by the authorised person but by other members of the same group or partnership of which it is a member. This is to ensure that the duties in subsection (1) of new sections 139B and 139C include a duty to make rules requiring a recovery or resolution plan, as the case may be, to include specified information relating to action to be taken by other members of the group or partnership of which the authorised person is a member. For this purpose, the wide meaning of "group" in section 421(1) of FSMA is narrowed by *subsection (2)* to exclude entities of which the authorised person (or other members of its group) may not necessarily have majority ownership or control.

97. *Subsection (3)* sets out some of the scenarios that constitute 'failure' of an authorised person for the purposes of new section 139C which the FSA may require to be covered in a resolution plan.

98. *Subsection (4)* widens the potential scope of a recovery or resolution plan by providing that the references in section 139B (see subsections (3) and (4)) and section 139C (see subsection (3)) to the "business" of the authorised person include the business of other persons in its group (including a holding company) or a partnership of which it is a member.

99. *Subsection (5)* provides that the term "specified" which is used in new sections 139B and C, means "specified" in general rules made by the FSA.

100. *Subsection (6)* makes clear that the references in new section 139D to "insolvency" and "administration" include the new procedures in Parts 2 and 3 respectively of the Banking Act 2009.

139E Rules about recovery and resolution plans: supplementary provision

101. *Subsection (1)* clarifies that the FSA can specify in its rules on RRPs that a resolution or recovery plan should set out the action which the authorised person is to take to collect, and maintain up-to-date, information of a specified description. This is to ensure that rules may require an authorised person quickly to establish and maintain a 'data room', which contains adequate data for interested third parties to perform due diligence on all or parts of the business, should circumstances require a sale.

102. Subsection (2) ensures that that where the FSA considers that an authorised person has failed to comply with the requirement referred to in subsection (1), the FSA may require the authorised person to appoint a skilled person to collect, and maintain up-to-date, the information that is needed.

103. *Subsection (3)* aligns the definition of a 'skilled person' with that of the existing section 166 of FSMA on 'skilled persons'.

104. *Subsection (4)* enables the 'skilled person' to require others to assist in the collection or updating of information. That requirement may be enforced in the manner described in *subsection (5)*.

105. To prepare a recovery or resolution plan an authorised person is likely to need to obtain information from persons connected to it and others. *Subsection (6)* facilitates the flow of information to the authorised person for the purposes of preparing a recovery or resolution plan from other parties, for example other parties in the group, or persons such as service providers. This subsection enables other parties, where the request or requirement to provide information has been approved in advance by the FSA, to disclose information relevant to preparing or maintaining a recovery or resolution plan to the authorised person without being in breach of any duty or obligation of confidence (whether imposed by contract or otherwise).

106. *Subsection (7)* clarifies the extent of the confidentiality obligations of an authorised person that receives confidential information under new section 139E(6) or already holds such information. The provision makes clear that an authorised person may, for example, include such information in its recovery or resolution plan and submit it to the FSA without having to seek the consent of a third party. *Paragraph 26 of Schedule 2* amends section 348(5)(d) of FSMA so that a skilled person appointed under new section 139E is treated in the same way as a person appointed to make a report under section 166 of FSMA.

107. *Subsection (8)* enables the FSA to require RRPs to be kept in electronic or any other format.

108. *Subsection (9)* sets out that, when making rules about RRPs, the FSA must also have regard to any internationally agreed standards on RRPs, including, but not limited to, the standards being developed by the Financial Stability Board ("FSB"). The FSB, through its Working Group on Cross-border Crisis Management, is piloting an internationally agreed template for RRPs on the major firms with cross-border crisis management groups and the template, redeveloped in line with the outcome of the pilot, will form the basis of the internationally agreed standards for RRPs, which are expected by the end of 2010.

New section 139F – Special provision in relation to resolution plans

109. *Subsection (1)* requires the FSA to consult the Treasury and the FSA about the adequacy of resolution plans required to be prepared by general rules so far as those plans relate to any matter which may be relevant to the exercise by the Treasury or Bank of England of any power under Part 1, 2 or 3 of the Banking Act 2009.

110. Under *subsection (2)* the Treasury or the Bank of England may, after that consultation, notify the FSA that, in their opinion, a resolution plan fails to make satisfactory provision in relation to any such matter and, if they do so, must give their reasons.

111. *Subsection (3)* requires the FSA to have regard to any notification given under subsection (2).

112. *Subsection (4)* requires the FSA, if it receives a notification under subsection (2) but considers that the resolution plan makes satisfactory provision, to give reasons for its opinion to the person who gave the notification.

113. Section 7(2) of the Act enables the Treasury, by order, to specify a date by which the FSA must make rules requiring authorised persons of a description specified in the order to prepare recovery or resolution plans. This subsection enables the Treasury to provide for a staged approach by making different orders in relation to authorised persons of different descriptions. Before making an order the Treasury is required under subsection (3) to consult the FSA. Subsection (4) provides that any order will be subject to the negative resolution procedure.

Short selling

Section 8: Power of FSA to prohibit, or require disclosure of, short selling

114. This section inserts a new Part 8A into FSMA, consisting of ten new sections (sections 131B to 131K). These sections provide the FSA with a new power to prohibit, or require disclosure of, short selling.

New section 131B: short selling rules

115. *Subsection (1)* provides that the FSA may make rules banning short selling in relation to certain financial instruments by prohibiting persons from engaging in this practice. These rules would apply to all persons, whether authorised by the FSA or not. These powers would not enable the FSA to ban a single firm from short selling a particular financial instrument while permitting other firms to do so.

116. *Subsection (2)* provides that the FSA may make rules requiring the disclosure of information relating to short selling in relation to specified financial instruments. This disclosure regime would apply to all persons, whether authorised by the FSA or not, who have engaged in short selling.

117. *Subsection (3)* sets out some of the provisions that may be included by the FSA in rules establishing a disclosure regime for short selling, in particular, when disclosures are to be made and the way in which disclosures are to be made.

118. *Subsection (4)* ensures that the FSA is able to obtain information about short selling which has taken place before the rules are made where the person concerned still has a short position when the rules are made. This will occur, for example, when the short seller (S) has sold financial instruments which S did not own, and has not at the time the rules are made purchased the instruments concerned in order to deliver them to the buyer or return them to the lender (if the sale was settled with borrowed instruments), and so closed out the short position or otherwise reduced their short position to a level below the disclosure threshold specified by the FSA.

*These notes refer to the Financial Services Act 2010 (c.28)
which received Royal Assent on 8 April 2010*

119. *Subsection (5)* ensures that, where there is any doubt, what is meant by "a short position being open" will be determined in accordance with the FSA's short selling rules.

120. *Subsection (6)* makes it clear that rules under this section may apply in relation to short selling taking place wholly outside the UK by persons outside the UK, but only in relation to financial instruments admitted to trading on markets in the UK. FSA rules may also apply to short selling:

    - by any person in the UK (including persons temporarily in the UK), or

    - through an intermediary present in the UK, or

    - in relation to shares admitted to trading in the UK (even if dual or multi-listed elsewhere in the world).

121. *Subsection (7)* allows the short selling rules described in this Part to be targeted at a particular form of financial instrument issued by a specified company.

122. *Subsection (8)* provides that rules made under section 131B are referred to as "short selling rules".

123. *Subsection (9)* requires the FSA to take account of any international agreement on short selling measures when it makes any rules in relation to short selling.

New section 131C: Short selling rules: definitions etc

124. This section defines the terms used in section 131B.

125. *Subsection (2)* defines short selling for the purposes of the short selling rules. Short selling will include any case in which a person sells a financial instrument which that person does not own, and will make a profit if the price of that instrument falls before the person has to buy the instrument to deliver it to the buyer or to return to the lender (where the sale was settled with borrowed financial instruments). It will also include any case in which a person enters into a transaction in a different financial instrument to the shorted instrument (whether the first-mentioned financial instrument was in existence before the transaction, or was created as a result of the transaction), where the effect of the transaction entered into is that that person will make a profit if there is a fall in value in the shorted instrument. For example, S may buy an equity put option giving S the right to sell 1,000 shares in ABC plc for £10 a share. If the price of the shares falls to £5, S will be able to buy 1,000 shares in the market for £5,000, exercise the option and sell the same shares for £10,000, making a profit of gross £5,000. Alternatively, S may enter into a contract for difference ("CFD") which provides that S will pay to B the difference between the current value of a financial instrument and its value at the date on which the contract for difference matures if the price increases (if the price falls, B pays the difference to S). The transaction will create a financial instrument (the CFD) and S will have engaged in short selling the

financial instrument to which the CFD relates because he will make a profit if the value of the financial instrument falls before that date.

126. *Subsections (3)* and *(4)* define "financial instrument" and "relevant financial instrument". *Subsections (5)* and *(6)* contain supplementary definitions. The definition of "relevant financial instrument" ensures that the FSA may make rules regulating short selling in relation to financial instruments admitted to trading in EEA markets, or which have any other connection to EEA markets which may be specified in the rules, as well as financial instruments admitted to trading in the UK.

127. *Subsection (7)* ensures that where a financial instrument is admitted to trading both on a UK or EEA market and markets elsewhere in the world the FSA may make short selling rules in relation to that instrument on any or all of the markets on which it is admitted to trading. Under *subsection (8)* the same applies where related financial instruments are admitted respectively to trading on an EEA market and a market elsewhere in the world. An instrument will be related for these purposes if the price or value of one instrument depends on the price or value of the other, as would be the case in relation to an equity share and a depositary receipt issued in relation to that share.

128. *Subsection (9)* defines "regulated market". *Subsection (10)* clarifies the meaning of references to a "market" in a particular territory.

New section 131D: Short selling rules: procedure in urgent cases

129. New section 131D provides for the procedure to be followed by the FSA where the FSA is making urgent restrictions on engaging in short selling.

130. *Subsection (1)* gives the FSA the power to make short selling rules, and subsequently to amend those rules, without going through the normal consultation process, where it is necessary to do so to protect the stability of the financial system, or to maintain confidence in the financial system.

131. *Subsection (2)* provides that initially these emergency short selling rules may last for no more than three months. However, under *subsections (3)* and *(4)* the FSA is given power to extend these rules for a further three months provided that it still considers them to be necessary to protect the stability of the financial system or to maintain confidence in the financial system at the time when the direction is given. Under *subsection (5)*, this direction must be published.

132. *Subsection (6)* provides that nothing prevents the FSA from revoking emergency rules before the end of the periods referred to in subsections (2) or (3).

New section 131E: Power to require information

133. This section gives the FSA a power to require the production of information or documents in order to ascertain whether there has been a breach of any short selling rules.

134. Subsection *(1)* gives the FSA the power to require information or documents to be produced. This applies whether or not the person concerned is an "authorised person" under FSMA. *Subsection (2)* sets out the scope of this power – the FSA may only impose such a requirement on a person if the information or documents are required in order to enable the FSA to determine whether that person or any person connected to that person, has breached any provision of the short selling rules.

135. *Subsections (3)* to *(5)* allow the FSA to specify the time and form in which the information must be provided. They may also require the person providing the information to take reasonable steps specified by the FSA to verify the information provided. *Subsection (7)* defines what is meant by a "connected person" for the purpose of this section.

New section 131F: Power to require information: supplementary

136. This section contains provisions corresponding to the provisions of section 175 of FSMA.

137. *Subsection (1)* enables the FSA to compel the production of a document by a person who is holding a document on behalf of another person if they would have the power to compel the latter to produce the document under new section 131E. Under *subsection (2)* a document, once obtained under new section 131E, may be copied or have extracts taken from it, and the person producing the document, or any other relevant person, may be required to explain it. *Subsection (3)* defines "relevant person" for these purposes.

138. Under *subsection (4)*, if any person required to produce a document fails to do so, they may be compelled to state where, to the best of their knowledge, the document is. Under *subsection (5)* lawyers may be compelled to provide the name and address of their clients.

139. Under *subsection (6)* documents subject to banking confidentiality may be withheld unless the person holding the information, or the person to whom the duty of confidence is owed, is the person under investigation or a related company, or the person to whom the duty is owed consents to its disclosure. *Subsection (7) provides that* the production of a document does not affect any lien a third party may have over it.

New section 131G: Power to impose penalty or issue censure

140. *Subsections (1) to (3)* set out the penalty for contravention of the short selling rules, or failure to comply with an information requirement imposed under new section 131E, or new section 131F. The FSA may impose an unlimited fine on any person, whether or not that person is an authorised person, if it is satisfied that the person has contravened any part of the short selling rules or an information requirement. The FSA may alternatively decide not to impose a fine, but to publish a statement of censure instead.

*These notes refer to the Financial Services Act 2010 (c.28)
which received Royal Assent on 8 April 2010*

141. *Subsections (4) to (6)* impose a three-year time limit on the FSA's ability to take such enforcement action against a person, unless, before the end of the three-year period, the FSA has given a warning notice to the person concerned under section 131H. The three-year period within which the FSA can act begins with the first day that the FSA knew that a person contravened any provision of the short selling rules or the information requirement.

New section 131H: Procedure and right to refer to Tribunal

142. *Subsections (1) to (3)* provide that a person must be given a warning notice detailing the amount of the fine or the terms of the public censure (as applicable) if the FSA proposes to take action against them.

143. *Subsections (4) to (6)* provide that a person must be given a decision notice detailing the amount of the fine or the terms of the public censure (as applicable) if the FSA decides to take action against them.

144. *Subsection (7)* provides that a person may refer the matter to the Tribunal if the FSA decides to take action against them.

New section 131I: Duty on publication of statement

145. This section requires the FSA to send a copy of any public censure to the person concerned and to any other person who was given a copy of the decision notice.

New section 131J: Imposition of penalties under section 131G: statement of policy

146. This section requires the FSA to issue a statement of its policy in relation to the imposition and amount of penalties. The policy set out in the statement must take account of the factors set out in *subsection (2)*.

147. Under *subsection (3)* the FSA is given power to alter or replace the statement of policy. If it does so, it must, under *subsection (4)*, issue the revised statement.

148. *Subsections (5) and (6)* require the FSA to give the Treasury a copy of any statement of policy it publishes, and to publish the statement so as to ensure that it is brought to public attention.

149. *Subsection (7)* enables the FSA to charge a fee for providing a copy of the statement of policy.

150. *Subsection (8)* requires the FSA to have regard to the statement in force at the time of the misconduct when imposing penalties under new section 131G.

New section 131K: Statement of policy: procedure

151. This section sets out the procedure for issuing a statement under new section 131J. Before deciding on its policies, or changing those policies, the FSA will be required to consult the public on its proposals.

*These notes refer to the Financial Services Act 2010 (c.28)
which received Royal Assent on 8 April 2010*

FSA's disciplinary powers

Section 9: Suspending permission to carry on regulated activities etc

152. Sections 205 and 206 of FSMA set out the disciplinary measures available to the FSA in respect of a contravention by an authorised person of a requirement imposed by or under FSMA or a directly applicable EU regulation made under the markets in financial instruments directive.

153. This section inserts a new section 206A into FSMA providing the FSA with additional sanctions to deal with such breaches. Those additional sanctions are the power to suspend, limit or otherwise restrict an authorised person's permission for up to a maximum of 12 months.

154. The section permits the FSA to impose one or more of the available sanctions in respect of the same contravention.

155. Sections 207 and 208 of FSMA set out the procedure for taking disciplinary measures, namely a warning notice followed by a decision notice and right of referral to the Tribunal. *Paragraphs 18 and 19 of Schedule 2* make consequential amendments to those sections to apply the same procedure to the imposition of the new sanctions.

156. Section 210 of FSMA requires the FSA to issue a statement of policy regarding the imposition of a financial penalty under section 206. *Paragraph 20 of Schedule 2* makes a consequential amendment to that section so that the statement of policy must also cover the length of any suspensions or restrictions imposed under the new s206A.

Section 10: Removal of restriction on imposing a penalty and cancelling authorisation

157. Section 206(2) of FSMA prohibits the FSA from both imposing a penalty on an authorised person under that section and withdrawing a person's authorisation under section 33 in respect of the same contravention. This section repeals this prohibition thus enabling the FSA to stop an authorised person from continuing to carry on a regulated activity at the same time as imposing a financial penalty on that person.

Section 11: Performance of controlled function without approval

158. Section 59 of FSMA requires an authorised person ('A') to take reasonable care to ensure that no person ('P') performs a controlled function under an arrangement entered into by A or A's contractor in relation to the carrying on by A of a regulated activity, unless P has been approved by the FSA to do so. There is currently no prohibition on a person performing a controlled function without FSA approval.

159. This section inserts new sections 63A to 63D into FSMA. New section 63A(1) enables the FSA to impose a financial penalty on a person if it is satisfied that that person has performed a controlled function without approval and that the person knew or could reasonably be expected to have known that he or she was performing a controlled function without approval.

160. New section 63B sets out the procedure for imposing a financial penalty, namely issuing a warning notice followed by a decision notice. There is a right of referral to the Tribunal.

161. New section 63C requires the FSA is required to consult on and publish a statement of its policy on the imposition of penalties and the amount of such penalties.

162. New section 63D sets out the procedure to be followed by the FSA before issuing such a policy statement.

163. Section 168 of FSMA enables the FSA to carry out investigations in particular cases, including the circumstances listed in subsection (4). *Paragraph 16 of Schedule 2* makes a consequential amendment to subsection (4) to provide for the FSA to appoint an investigator if it thinks that a person may have performed a controlled function without approval.

Section 12: Approved persons guilty of misconduct

164. Section 66 of FSMA sets out the FSA's disciplinary powers in respect of misconduct by approved persons. Approved persons are persons who have approval from the FSA to carry out controlled functions. Controlled functions are set out in FSA rules and include, for example, having responsibility for compliance with FSA rules or being a director.

165. This section amends section 66 of FSMA to add to the current sanctions (financial penalty and public censure) that the FSA can impose for misconduct. It enables the FSA to suspend an approved person from carrying on certain functions, and / or impose restrictions on that person's performance of certain functions, for a maximum period of 2 years.

166. Paragraphs 9 and 10 of Schedule 2 make consequential amendments to sections 67 (disciplinary measures: procedure and right to refer to Tribunal) and 69 (statements of policy) so that they apply to the new sanctions.

167. *Subsection (4)* amends section 66(4) to increase the limitation period on the FSA taking disciplinary action against an approved person from two to three years.

Section 13: Publication of decision notices

168. This section amends section 391 of FSMA, which establishes common rules on publication of notices by the Authority, to widen the categories of supervisory notices that may be published.

169. *Subsection (2)* removes the prohibition on the publication of decision notices.

170. *Subsection (3)* inserts a new subsection (1A) which provides that the person to whom a decision notice is given may only publish such details of the notice as the FSA has published.

171. *Subsection (4)* amends section 391(4) to require the FSA to publish such information about decision notices (as well as final notices) as it considers appropriate. This new requirement will be subject to section 391(6).

Measures to protect consumers

Section 14: Consumer redress schemes

172. The existing section 404 of FSMA enables the Treasury, subject to Parliamentary approval, to authorise the FSA to require firms to conduct a review of past business and, if liable, to pay compensation to consumers. Section 14 replaces section 404 with new sections 404 and 404A to 404G, conferring new powers for the FSA to make rules requiring firms to establish and operate consumer redress schemes.

New section 404: Consumer redress schemes

173. *Subsections (1)* and *(3)* provide that the FSA may make section 404 rules if it appears to it that (a) there may have been a widespread or regular failure by a relevant firm (defined in *subsection (2)*) as an authorised person or payment service provider) to comply with the requirements for carrying on an activity; (b) as a result, consumers have suffered or may suffer loss for which redress would be available in legal proceedings; and (c) it is desirable to establish a scheme to secure redress for consumers.

174. 'Consumers' is defined in new section 404E.

175. New section 404F(5) provides that references to a relevant firm include a person who was, but is no longer, an authorised person or payment service provider and a person who has assumed a liability incurred by a relevant firm.

176. *Subsections (4)* to *(7)* of new section 404 define 'consumer redress scheme' as one in which a firm is required to take one or more of the following steps:

- investigate whether it has failed to comply with its obligations in carrying out a specified activity;

- if it determines that it has failed to comply with an obligation, determine the nature and extent of the failure, and whether the failure has caused or may cause any loss to consumers;

- if it determines that consumers have suffered loss, to make appropriate redress.

New section 404A: Rules under section 404: supplementary

177. Section 404A sets out matters for which section 404 rules may make provision. This includes requiring firms to provide the FSA with information about their investigation and the matters under investigation, and for the FSA (or a competent person appointed by it) to conduct the investigation and other relevant steps instead of the firm,

including determining its liability and the redress the firm should make to consumers. Where the rules provide for a scheme to be conducted by someone other than the firm itself, they must also include provision for warning and decision notices and a right of referral to the Tribunal *(subsection (8))*.

178. *Subsection (2)* limits the FSA's power in *subsection (1)(b)* to define by way of example what amounts to a failure to comply with a requirement to that which a court has found or would find constitutes a failure. *Subsection (3)* similarly limits the FSA's power in *subsection (1)(c)* to set out matters which should be taken into account by firms in assessing evidence or determining causation to those matters which a court has taken, or would take, into account. *Subsection (4)* provides that the FSA may require firms to make such redress as is just in relation to that description of case, having regard (among other things) to the nature and extent of the losses in question. It is not limited to the remedy or relief which would be available in legal proceedings.

New section 404B: Complaints to the ombudsman scheme

179. This section enables a consumer who is not satisfied with any determination by a firm under a scheme to make a complaint to the Financial Ombudsman Service (FOS). It requires the FOS to assess such a complaint (or a complaint about an underlying act or omission which falls to be dealt with by a consumer redress scheme) in accordance with the terms of the consumer redress scheme rather than its 'fair and reasonable' jurisdiction under section 226(8) of FSMA. Complaints under this section will form part of the FOS' compulsory jurisdiction set out in Schedule 17 to FSMA.

New section 404C: Enforcement

180. This section provides that the FSA's disciplinary powers in Part 14 of FSMA (public censure or financial penalty) will apply to relevant firms which are not (or no longer) authorised persons. This ensures that the scheme can be enforced against payment service providers or firms which are no longer authorised.

New section 404D: Applications to Tribunal to quash rules or provision of rules

181. This section enables a person to apply to the Tribunal for a review of any rules made by the FSA under section 404. The general rule is that the Tribunal is to apply judicial review principles to such applications. On an application relating to an example set out in the rules of things done or omitted which firms are to regard as constituting a failure to comply with a requirement (under section 404A(1)(b)) the Tribunal may determine whether the example does in fact constitute a failure. On an application relating to matters the FSA requires firms to take into account for the purpose of assessing evidence or determining causation under section 404A(1)(c)), the Tribunal may determine whether, in its view, these are matters that firms should be required to take into account. The section gives the Tribunal jurisdiction to quash any rules made under section 404 or any provision of those rules.

*These notes refer to the Financial Services Act 2010 (c.28)
which received Royal Assent on 8 April 2010*

New section 404G: Power to widen the scope of consumer redress schemes

182. This section gives the Treasury a power to widen the scope of the FSA's power to establish a consumer redress scheme by amending the definition of relevant firms or consumers.

Section 15: Restrictions on provision of credit card cheques

183. This section inserts new sections 51A and 51B into the Consumer Credit Act 1974. New section 51A makes it an offence for a credit card issuer to send credit card cheques to a customer other than in response to a request from that customer.

184. The request may be entirely at the instigation of the customer or the credit card issuer may offer to send cheques (for example via a mail shot). However, the customer cannot be considered to have requested cheques simply because he has not said he does not want them. The credit card issuer may not send more than three cheques to a customer in response to a request (but must send fewer than three if requested). The customer cannot make an ongoing request, for example, he cannot ask for one cheque per month for the next year or indefinitely. The restrictions on meeting requests apply at the level of the agreement rather than the customer, so the customer can request and be sent cheques on more than one card at the same time.

185. Credit card cheques are provided by many credit card issuers to those to whom they have issued credit cards. They are very similar in appearance to ordinary bank current account cheques and can be used in any situation where a current account cheque can be used (but they are not guaranteed by the credit card as a current account cheque is guaranteed by a cheque guarantee card). Once used, the cheque appears on the credit card statement in the same way as an item purchased with the card or a cash withdrawal on the card. In the new section 51A, credit card cheques are defined by reference to the provision of credit under a credit-token agreement. A credit-token agreement is defined in section 14 of the Consumer Credit Act 1974 as a regulated agreement to provide credit in connection with the use of a credit-token. Credit-tokens include credit cards.

186. New section 51B provides that new section 51A does not apply to credit card cheques issued to business customers.

Financial Services Compensation Scheme

187. The FSCS is the scheme established by the FSA under Part 15 of FSMA to compensate customers of authorised persons when they firms are in default, that is, unable or likely to be unable to pay claims.

Section 16: Contribution to costs of special resolution regime

188. This section inserts new sections 214B, 214C and 214D into FSMA to replace the existing section 214B (inserted by section 171 of the Banking Act 2009).

189. Existing section 214B confers a power on the Treasury to require the Financial Services Compensation Scheme ("the FSCS") to contribute to the costs incurred in applying the stabilisation powers of the special resolution regime ("the SRR") (established in Part 1 of the Banking Act 2009) to a bank that is failing. The amount that the FSCS can be required to contribute is limited to the amount of compensation that the FSCS would have had to pay to depositors if the failing bank had entered into insolvency (i.e. if the SRR powers had not been used), net of any amounts the FSCS would have recovered in that insolvency. The section provides for an independent valuer to be appointed to calculate this likely amount of recovery.

190. New sections 214B to 214D restate the provisions of existing section 214B with corrections and clarifications, and make provision for the calculation of amounts owed by the FSCS. *Subsection (2)* of section 16 provides for the amended provisions to apply with retrospective effect from 19 November 2009 (the date of introduction of this Act) to allow interest to be taken into account in calculating FSCS contributions from that date onwards in cases where a stabilisation power was exercised before the commencement of this section.

191. New section 214B allows the Treasury to include interest costs in the calculation of expenses incurred in connection with the exercise of the stabilisation power. *Subsection (6)* provides for the Treasury to set the rate at which that interest is to be calculated and the interest rate to be used in calculating the maximum amount the FSCS may be required to contribute.

192. New section 214C provides for the maximum amount that the FSCS may be required to contribute. This is limited to the notional net expenditure, which is the amount that the FSCS would have paid in the hypothetical scenario where the stabilisation power had not been exercised and the bank had entered insolvency proceedings, minus the actual net expenditure (i.e. any actual payments the FSCS has made in respect of the resolution, net of any recoveries made). *Subsections (5)* and (6) allow for interest to be taken into account in calculating this expenditure.

193. New section 214D makes further provision supplementing new sections 214B and 214C. New provisions include an express obligation on the FSCS to calculate the amount and the timing of compensation payments in the hypothetical scenario; provision for appointment of an independent valuer to calculate the timings of recoveries likely to be made by the FSCS in that scenario and provision for the Treasury to specify principles to be taken into account by the independent valuer and the FSCS when making such calculations. *Subsection (6)* extends the existing subsection 214B(3)(b) by providing for independent verification of other matters as well as the expenses incurred in section 214B(2). *Subsections (8)* and *(9)* make revised provision for the situation when the FSCS is required to contribute to the costs of resolution before the end of the resolution.

*These notes refer to the Financial Services Act 2010 (c.28)
which received Royal Assent on 8 April 2010*

Section 17: Power to require FSCS manager to act in relation to other schemes

194. This section, which inserts new Part 15A into FSMA (comprising sections 224B to 224F), extends the scope of the FSCS manager's powers to enable it to make payments on behalf of another compensation scheme or arrangement that pays compensation in respect of institutions that provide financial services, including institutions that are not authorised persons under FSMA.

195. New section 224B defines the terms used, including the kinds of scheme or arrangement under which the Treasury can require the FSCS manager to act on behalf of another person paying compensation to customers of financial services firms ("the relevant scheme"). *Subsection (9)* makes clear that the provisions of new Part 15A apply equally in cases where the relevant scheme is operated by the UK Government. New section 224C provides that if compensation is payable under a relevant scheme, the Treasury may issue a notice requiring the FSCS manager to act on behalf of the relevant scheme's manager. The notice will specify the functions to be performed by the FSCS manager on behalf of the manager of the relevant scheme.

196. Section 224D provides that the FSCS manager may decline to act if a ground in section 224E is met, and a notice to this effect is given to the Treasury. The grounds are: where the FSCS manager is not satisfied that it will be able to obtain the necessary information, advice or assistance from the administrator to comply with the notice; where it is not satisfied that funding is being provided to meet the expenditure that it will incur in acting on behalf of the relevant scheme manager; where it is of the opinion that complying with the notice would detrimentally affect the exercise of its FSCS functions; where the manager of the relevant scheme has not given an undertaking not to bring proceedings against the FSCS manager; or where there are no arrangements for the reimbursement of expenses arising out of claims brought against the FSCS manager by third parties.

197. New section 224F enables the FSA to make rules in connection with FSCS manager acting as a paying agent on behalf of relevant schemes. This includes conferring a power on the FSCS manager to impose levies to cover its expenses under this section; however if the FSA do impose such a power, it may be exercised only if the FSCS manager has tried and failed to obtain reimbursement of its expenses elsewhere.

Powers to require information

Section 18: Information relating to financial stability

198. This section inserts new sections 165A-165C and 169A into FSMA providing the FSA with new powers to require a person to provide specified information.

New section 165A: Authority's power to require information: financial stability

199. *Subsection (1)* provides that the FSA may, by giving written notice, require that a person provides the FSA with information or documents described in the notice.

200. Subsection *(2)* sets out the categories of people who may be required to provide information or documents under subsection (1). They include the owners or managers of investment funds and any persons connected to them. Section 165A(2)(d) confers on the Treasury a power to prescribe further categories of persons in respect of which the power under section 165A(1) may be exercised.

201. Subsection *(3)* sets out the test which will enable the FSA to require information: the FSA must consider that the information or documents in question are or might be, relevant to the stability of one or more aspects of the financial system.

202. Subsection *(4)* provides an additional test where a requirement is being imposed on a service provider or a person who is connected with a service provider. In this case, no requirement may be imposed unless the FSA considers that a failure by the provider to provide all or part of the services is likely to pose a serious threat to the stability of the financial system.

203. Subsection *(5)* gives the FSA power to determine the place at which, and the time within which, the information must be provided. The FSA must allow a reasonable period for the provision of the information.

204. Subsection *(6)* gives the FSA power to determine the form in which information must be provided to them.

205. Subsection *(7)* gives the FSA power to require any information provided to be verified or authenticated, by, for example, a firm's auditors.

206. Subsection *(8)* and (9) defines "relevant investment fund" for the purposes of this section, and sets out the other definitions used.

207. Subsection *(10)* defines "connected person" for the purposes of this section. .

New section 165B: Safeguards etc in relation to exercise of power under section 165A

208. This section sets out the procedural safeguards which will apply to the exercise of the power in new section 165A. Under *subsection (1)* the FSA must give a person on whom it proposes to impose a requirement written notice in advance.

209. Under *subsection (2)* the written notice must give the FSA's reasons for proposing to impose the requirement; and specify a reasonable timescale within which the person may make representations to the FSA. Once this period has expired, the FSA must, under *subsection (3)* decide within a reasonable period whether the requirement should be imposed.

210. Subsection *(4)* provides that subsections (1), (2) and (3) do not apply where the FSA is satisfied that it is necessary for the information to be provided urgently.

211. Subsection *(5)* requires the FSA to give its reasons when it imposes a requirement under this section.

212. *Subsection (6)* requires the FSA to prepare a statement of its policy with respect to the exercise of the power conferred by section 165A. Under *subsections (7)* and *(8)* this statement requires the approval of the Treasury and must be published. Under *subsection (9)*, this power may not be exercised before the statement has been approved and published.

New section 165C: Orders under section 165A(2)(d)

213. Section 165C sets out the conditions under which the Treasury may exercise the power given in section 165A(2)(d) to add a further category of persons who may be required to provide information under section 165A, and the procedure to be followed. Under *subsection (1)* the Treasury may only make such an order if it considers that the activities carried on by the prescribed person or the failure to carry on those activities (or any part of them), might pose a serious threat to the stability of the financial system.

214. *Subsection (2)* provides the general rule that an order made under section 165A(2)(d) will be subject to the normal affirmative resolution procedure, being laid in draft and approved by a resolution of each House.

215. *Subsections (3) to (7)* provide, as an exception to this rule, that where the Treasury considers that it is necessary, an order under section 165A(2)(d) will be subject to a modified form of the affirmative resolution procedure under which it must be laid before Parliament after being made and ceases to have effect at the end of a period of 28 days unless it is approved by a resolution of each House before the end of that period.

216. *Subsection (8)* ensures that no order under section 165A(2)(d) will be treated as a hybrid instrument for the purposes of the Standing Orders of either House of Parliament.

New section 169A: Support of overseas regulator with respect to financial stability

217. *Subsection (1)* provides that the FSA may exercise a corresponding section 165A power at the request of an overseas regulator.

218. *Subsection (2)* defines "overseas regulator" for the purposes of this section.

219. *Subsection (3)* defines "corresponding section 165A power" as a modified form of the power given in section 165A, with references to the stability of the financial system referring to the financial system operating in the country, or in a territory (such as Gibraltar or the Channel Islands) of the overseas regulator, and the reference to the UK in section 165A being replaced by a reference to that country or territory.

220. *Subsection (4)* sets out which provisions of section 165A are to apply to the corresponding section 165A power given in relation to overseas regulators.

221. *Subsection (5)* defines "financial system" for the purposes of this section.

Section 19: Asset protection scheme etc

222. The Asset Protection Scheme (APS) was announced by the Treasury in January 2009. Under the terms of the APS the Treasury provides, in return for a fee, protection against future credit losses incurred by an eligible UK-incorporated authorised deposit-takers on one or more portfolios of defined assets.

223. This section gives the Treasury the power to require information or documents it reasonably requires from participants or proposed participants in the APS or related schemes ('qualifying schemes').

224. *Subsection (2)* defines the asset protection scheme as the scheme which was subject to a statement made by the Chancellor of the Exchequer to Parliament on 26 February 2009.

225. *Subsections (3) and (8)* enable the Treasury to specify in an order that this section applies to schemes that the Treasury considers correspond to, or are connected with, the asset protection scheme. The section also applies to information or documents required in relation to the agreements entered into with participants in connection with the asset protection scheme or a qualifying scheme (*subsection (4)*).

226. *Subsections (5) and (6)* allow the Treasury to specify when and where the information and documents should be provided, and the form the information should take.

227. The Treasury can seek to enforce the requirements under this section by way of an injunction, or in Scotland, by way of an order for specific performance.

Banking Act 2009

Section 20: Services forming part of recognised inter-bank payment systems

228. This section inserts a new section 206A into Part 5 of the Banking Act 2009 (the Act) (inter-bank payment systems).

New section 206A: Services forming part of recognised inter-bank payment systems

229. *Subsection (1)* confers a power on the Treasury to make order(s) applying (and modifying (*subsection (7)*)) any sections under Part 5 of the Act to "service providers". "Service providers" are defined in *subsection (2)* as persons who supply services (such as telecommunication and IT systems) that form part of the arrangements of an inter-bank payment system that is specified by the Treasury as a recognised system under section 184(1) of the Act. The Bank of England may not be regarded as a service provider (*subsection (5)*).

230. An order under *subsection (1)* may be made only after consultation (*subsection (6)*) and only if a draft has been approved by each House of Parliament (*subsection (8)*).

231. It is envisaged that any order made applying Part 5 to service providers would make provision for the role of the FSA and the Bank of England in relation to persons who

are subject to the oversight of the FSA, either as a person who has a permission under Part 4 of FSMA, or is a recognised persons under Part 18 of that Act.

232. In the event an order is made applying provisions of Part 5 to service providers, the Treasury must specify in any recognition orders made under section 184 of the Act the service providers who are to be subject to the Bank of England's oversight under Part 5 of the Act (as applied) (*subsection (2(b)*). Before specifying any person as a service provider, the Treasury must consult with various parties, including the person whom the Treasury proposes to specify (*subsection (4)*).

Section 21: Minor amendments of provision made by Banking Act 2009

233. Parts 1 to 3 of the Act establish a permanent special resolution regime (SRR), providing the Authorities with tools to deal with banks and building societies that are failing to meet the conditions for authorisation to perform deposit-taking activities (and credit unions if applied by section 89 of that Act). This section makes technical amendments to certain provisions in Parts 1 to 3 and to a provision in Part 15 of FSMA (which was inserted by Part 4 of the Banking Act 2009).

234. The Act includes property transfer powers, which may be used to effect a transfer of some or all of the property, rights or liabilities of a failing institution; and to make provision for the purposes of, in connection with, or in consequence of such a transfer. *Subsection (2)* inserts a new section 48A (creation of liabilities) into the Act, expressly stating that this includes the power to create liabilities. This could be used, for example, where more liabilities than assets are transferred from a failing institution to a commercial purchaser and public funds are provided to make the transfer commercially viable. A liability may then be imposed on the residual of the failing institution in respect of these monies. New section 48A(2) makes clear that this liability can be determined by reference to another instrument such as an agreement with the transferee, which may make provision for the calculation of the amount of the liability.

235. The Act confers various powers on the Treasury to put in place compensation measures following an exercise of the stabilisation powers (see section 49), which may include provision for the appointment of independent valuers. These orders are subject to the affirmative procedure. The Treasury may make also additional provision for valuers, for example, their remuneration and procedure in separate orders, subject to the negative procedure. *Subsection (3)* allows for orders, subject to the affirmative procedure, that provide for the appointment of a valuer to contain this supplementary provision.

236. *Subsection (4)* makes a minor amendment to section 56 of the Act (independent valuer: money) providing a power for the Treasury to make provision for the payment of remuneration and allowances of persons appointed to remove an independent valuer from office, correcting an oversight in the Act.

*These notes refer to the Financial Services Act 2010 (c.28)
which received Royal Assent on 8 April 2010*

237. *Subsection (5)* provides that the Treasury can make a third party compensation order where a building society has been taken into temporary public ownership by way of a subscription to new deferred shares in the society, correcting an oversight in the Act.

238. Part 3 of the Act establishes a new bank administration procedure, which incorporates provisions of the Insolvency Act 1986 through a table listing all relevant sections, schedule and paragraphs that need to be included. *Subsection (6)* substitutes an entry relating to paragraph 79 of Schedule B1 of the Insolvency Act for the one relating to paragraph 80 of that Schedule. Paragraph 79 provides for the discharge of an administrator appointed by the court, and therefore is more apt for bank administration than paragraph 80, which provides for the discharge of an administrator appointed in other ways. *Subsection (7)* makes consequential changes to section 153 of the Act.

239. The Act inserts new sections into FSMA requiring the FSCS to contribute to special resolution regime costs and providing for information to be given to the FSCS in that case. Section 219(3A) of FSMA refers only to a "bank", although it is intended to refer to all the institutions subject to the special resolution regime i.e. banks, building societies and credit unions. *Subsection (8)* amends the provision so it refers to all of these institutions.

Director of Savings

Section 22: Administration of court funds by Director of Savings

240. This section provides for the Director of Savings to undertake functions on behalf of the Accountant General for England and Wales where appointed to do so under court funds rules. The rules in question are the court funds rules made under section 38(7) of the Administration of Justice Act 1982.

241. *Subsection (1)* defines the term "relevant function" for the purposes of this section as being a function of the Accountant General of the Senior Courts under court funds rules. *Subsection (4)* defines what is meant by the term "court funds rules". For these purposes, court funds rules are the rules as to the administration and management of funds in court made under section 38(7) of the Administration of Justice Act 1982. (The court funds rules currently in force are the Court Funds Rules 1987.)

242. *Subsection (2)* provides that the Director of Savings ("the Director") may carry out a relevant function if appointed by the Accountant General under court funds rules to do so. Section 38(8)(a) of the Administration of Justice Act 1982 provides that the court funds rules may enable the Accountant General to appoint a person or persons to discharge functions conferred on the Accountant General under the rules (i.e. functions relating to the administration and management of funds in court). This provision, therefore, enables the Director to carry out functions relating to the administration and management of funds in court where the Accountant General appoints the Director, under the court funds rules to do so.

243. *Subsection (3)* makes clear that the power of the Director, under the court funds rules, to carry out relevant functions falls within section 69(1)(a) of the Deregulation and Contracting Out Act 1994. This means that such power may be included in an order made under section 69(2) of that Act enabling the Director to contract out the power to such person as the Director may authorise to do so.

General

Section 23: Orders or regulations

244. This section contains provision about orders and regulations under the Act.

Section 24: Minor and consequential amendments

245. This section introduces *Schedule 2* and confers a power to make consequential amendments.

FINANCIAL EFFECTS OF THE ACT

246. The financial effects of this Act are minimal, and largely limited to the creation of the CFEB and Money Guidance. On indicative budget forecasts, the costs of the CFEB, including delivery of Money Guidance and projects which form part of the National Strategy for Financial Capability, could rise from £37 million in 2010-11 to £56 million in 2014-15. It is expected that the costs of the CFEB to decline slowly thereafter, once the Money Guidance service is at 'steady state'. The financial services industry, through a levy on FSA-regulated firms and OFT-licensed consumer credit firms, will provide the principal funding for the CFEB's activity. However, it is expected that the Government will pay up to half of the costs of the Money Guidance component of the CFEB's costs (up to £20 million by 2014-15) through dormant accounts funds and public funds.

COMMENCEMENT DATES

247. Section 26 sets out the provisions that come into force on Royal Assent, and the provisions that come into force two months after Royal Assent. The remaining provisions come into force on an appointed day.

These notes refer to the Financial Services Act 2010 (c.28) which received Royal Assent on 8 April 2010

HANSARD REFERENCES

248. The following table sets out the dates and Hansard references for each stage of this Act's passage through Parliament.

Stage	Date	Hansard Reference
House of Commons		
Introduction	19 November 2009	19 Nov 2009 : Column 142
Second Reading	30 November 2009	30 Nov 2009 : Column 872
Committee	8 December 2009 to 14 January 2010	Financial Services Bill Public Bill committee: 8 December 2009: Column number 1 8 December 2009: Column number: 27 10 December 2009: Column number: 69 10 December 2009: Column number: 91 15 December 2009: Column number: 115 15 December 2009: Column number: 153 5 January 2010: Column number: 187 5 January 2010: Column number: 225 7 January 2010: Column number: 273 7 January 2010: Column number: 295 12 January 2010 : Column number: 339 12 January 2010: Column number: 375 14 January 2010: Column number: 413 14 January 210: Column number: 437
Report and Third Reading	25 January 2010	25 Jan 2010 : Column 555 25 Jan 2010 : Column 641
House of Lords		
Introduction	25 January 2010	26 Jan 2010 : Column 1374
Second Reading	23 February 2010	23 Feb 2010 : Column 943
Committee	10 March 2010, 15 March 2010, 7 April 2010	10 Mar 2010 : Column 245 15 Mar 2010 : Column 502 7 Apr 2010 : Column 1504
Report and Third Reading	8 April 2010	8 Apr 2010 : Column 1663

These notes refer to the Financial Services Act 2010 (c.28) which received Royal Assent on 8 April 2010

House of Commons		
Commons consideration of Lords amendments	8 April 2010	8 Apr 2010 : Column 1242
Royal Assent	8 April 2010	House of Lords Hansard 8 Apr 2010 : Column 1738 House of Commons Hansard 8 Apr 2010 : Column 1256

ANNEX: LIST OF ABBREVIATIONS

APS – The Asset Protection Scheme

CCA – Consumer Credit Act 1974

CFEB – Consumer Financial Education Body

ECHR – European Convention on Human Rights

FSA – Financial Services Authority

FSCS – Financial Services Compensation Scheme

FSMA – Financial Services and Markets Act 2000

HMT – Her Majesty's Treasury

NS&I – National Savings and Investments

OFT – Office of Fair Trading

RRP – Recovery and Resolution Plan

the relevant authorities – The Treasury, FSA and Bank of England